EURIPIDES

Ion

Translated by
W. S. DI PIERO

Introduction, Notes, and Commentary by
PETER BURIAN

New York   Oxford
OXFORD UNIVERSITY PRESS
1996

Oxford University Press

Oxford   New York

Athens   Auckland   Bangkok   Bombay
Calcutta   Cape Town   Dar es Salaam   Delhi
Florence   Hong Kong   Istanbul   Karachi
Kuala Lumpur   Madras   Madrid   Melbourne
Mexico City   Nairobi   Paris   Singapore
Taipei   Tokyo   Toronto

and associated companies in
Berlin   Ibadan

Copyright © 1996 by W. S. Di Piero and Peter Burian

Published by Oxford University Press, Inc.
198 Madison Avenue, New York, New York 10016

Oxford is a registered trademark of Oxford University Press

All rights reserved. No part of this publication may be reproduced,
stored in a retrieval system, or transmitted, in any form or by any means,
electronic, mechanical, photocopying, recording, or otherwise,
without the prior permission of Oxford University Press.

Library of Congress Cataloging-in-Publication Data
Euripides.
[Ion. English]
Ion/Euripides; translated by W. S. Di Piero;
introduction, notes, and commentary by Peter Burian.
p.   cm. — (Greek tragedy in new translations)
ISBN 0-19-509451-4
1. Ion (Greek mythology)—Drama. I. Di Piero, W. S. II. Title.
III. Series.
PA3975.16D5   1996   882'.01—dc20
95-34977

9 8 7 6 5 4 3 2 1
Printed in the United States of America

EDITORS' FOREWORD

The Greek Tragedy in New Translations is based on the conviction that poets like Aeschylus, Sophocles, and Euripides can only be properly rendered by translators who are themselves poets. Scholars may, it is true, produce useful and perceptive versions. But our most urgent present need is for a *re-creation* of these plays—as though they had been written, freshly and greatly, by masters fully at home in the English of our own times. Unless the translator is a poet, his original is likely to reach us in crippled form: deprived of the power and pertinence it must have if it is to speak to us of what is permanent in the Greek. But poetry is not enough; the translator must obviously *know* what he is doing, or he is bound to do it badly. Clearly, few contemporary poets possess enough Greek to undertake the complex and formidable task of transplanting a Greek play without also "colonializing" it or stripping it of its deep cultural difference, its remoteness from us. And that means depriving the play of that crucial *otherness* of Greek experience—a quality no less valuable to us than its closeness. Collaboration between scholar and poet is therefore the essential operating principle of the series. In fortunate cases scholar and poet co-exist; elsewhere we have teamed able poets and scholars in an effort to supply, through affinity and intimate collaboration, the necessary combination of skills.

An effort has been made to provide the general reader or student with first-rate critical introductions, clear expositions of translators' principles, commentary on difficult passages, ample stage directions, and glossaries of mythical terms encountered in the plays. Our purpose throughout has been to make the reading of the plays as vivid as possible. But our poets have constantly tried to remember that they were translating *plays*—plays meant to be produced, in language that actors could speak, naturally and with dignity. The poetry aims at being *dramatic* poetry and realizing itself in words and actions that are both speakable and playable.

Finally, the reader should perhaps be aware that no pains have been spared in order that the "minor" plays should be translated as carefully and brilliantly as the acknowledged masterpieces. For the Greek Tragedy in New Translations aims to be, in the fullest sense, *new*. If we need vigorous new poetic versions, we also need to see the plays with fresh eyes, to reassess the plays *for ourselves,* in terms of our own needs. This means translations that liberate us from the canons of an earlier age because the translators have recognized, and discovered, in often neglected works, the perceptions and wisdom that make these works ours and necessary to us.

A NOTE ON THE SERIES FORMAT

If only for the illusion of coherence, a series of thirty-three Greek plays requires a consistent format. Different translators, each with his individual voice, cannot possibly develop the sense of a single coherent style for each of the three tragedians; nor even the illusion that, despite their differences, the tragedians share a common set of conventions and a generic, or period, style. But they can at least share a common approach to orthography and a common vocabulary of conventions.

1. Spelling of Greek Names

Adherence to the old convention whereby Greek names were first Latinized before being housed in English is gradually disappearing. We are now clearly moving away from Latinization and toward precise transliteration. The break with tradition may be regrettable, but there is much to be said for hearing and seeing Greek names as though they were both Greek and *new,* instead of Roman or neo-classical importations. We cannot of course see them as wholly new. For better or worse certain names and myths are too deeply rooted in our literature and thought to be dislodged. To speak of "Helene" and "Hekabe" would be no less pedantic and absurd than to write "Aischylos" or "Platon" or "Thoukydides." There are of course borderline cases. "Jocasta" (as opposed to "Iokaste") is not a major mythical figure in her own right; her familiarity in her Latin form is a function of the fame of Sophocles' play as the tragedy *par excellence.* And as tourists we go to Delphi, not Delphoi. The precisely transliterated form may be pedantically "right," but the pedantry goes against the grain of cultural habit and actual usage.

As a general rule, we have therefore adopted a "mixed" orthography according to the principles suggested above. When a name has been firmly housed in English (admittedly the question of domestication is often moot), the traditional spelling has been kept. Otherwise names have been translit-erated. Throughout the series the *-os* termination of masculine names has been adopted, and Greek diphthongs (as in Iphigene*ia*) have normally been retained. We cannot expect complete agreement from readers (or from translators, for that matter) about borderline cases. But we want at least to make the operative principle clear: to walk a narrow line between orthographical extremes in the hope of keeping what should not, if possible, be lost; and refreshing, in however tenuous a way, the specific sound and name-boundedness of Greek experience.

2. Stage directions

The ancient manuscripts of the Greek plays do not supply stage directions (though the ancient commentators often provide information relevant to staging, delivery, "blocking," etc.). Hence stage directions must be inferred from words and situations and our knowledge of Greek theatrical conventions. At best this is a ticklish and uncertain procedure. But it is surely preferable that good stage directions should be provided by the translator than that the reader should be left to his own devices in visualizing action, gesture, and spectacle. Obviously the directions supplied should be both spare and defensible. Ancient tragedy was austere and "distanced" by means of masks, which means that the reader must not expect the detailed intimacy ("He shrugs and turns wearily away," "She speaks with deliberate slowness, as though to emphasize the point," etc.) which characterizes stage directions in modern naturalistic drama. Because Greek drama is highly rhetorical and stylized, the translator knows that his words must do the real work of inflection and nuance. Therefore every effort has been made to supply the visual and tonal sense required by a given scene and the reader's (or actor's) putative unfamiliarity with the ancient conventions.

3. Numbering of lines

For the convenience of the reader who may wish to check the English against the Greek text or vice versa, the lines have been numbered according to both the Greek text and the translation. The lines of the English translation have been numbered in multiples of ten, and these numbers have been set in the right-hand margin. The (inclusive) Greek numeration will be found bracketed at the top of the page. The reader will doubtless note that in many plays the English lines out-number the Greek, but he should not therefore conclude that the translator has been unduly prolix. In most cases the reason is simply that the translator has adopted the free-flowing norms of modern Anglo-American prosody, with its brief, breath- and emphasis-determined lines, and its habit of indicating cadence and caesuras by line length and setting rather than by conventional punctuation. Other translators have preferred four-beat or five-beat lines, and in these cases Greek and English numerations will tend to converge.

4. Notes and Glossary

In addition to the Introduction, each play has been supplemented by Notes (identified by the line numbers of the translation) and a Glossary. The Notes are meant to supply information which the translators deem important to the interpretation of a passage; they also afford the translator an opportunity to justify what he has done. The Glossary is intended to spare the reader the trouble of going elsewhere to look up mythical or geographical terms. The entries are not meant to be comprehensive; when a fuller explanation is needed, it will be found in the Notes.

Boston   WILLIAM ARROWSMITH AND HERBERT GOLDER

CONTENTS

ION

INTRODUCTION

I

The *Ion* is one of those plays of Euripides that refuses to stay put. Is it a savage attack on Apollo and traditional Greek religion? a celebration of Athens' divine origins and imperial destiny? or a sophisticated and disenchanted comedy of ideas? It has been claimed as all these things and more. Although the various readings seem fundamentally incompatible, none can simply be dismissed as without textual foundation. But attempts to fix the play's meaning by reference to a religious or political thesis or even to escapism dictated by the hard times in Athens around 410 B.C.[1] are inevitably reductive. Even a cursory glance at the action is enough to suggest what disturbing riptides of thought and feeling run just below the shimmering surface of Euripidean melodrama.

Kreousa, queen of Athens, and Xouthos, her foreign husband, arrive at Delphi to ask Apollo's help in ending their childlessness. The god, however, had long ago raped Kreousa and left her with a son whom she bore in secret and abandoned. Unbeknownst to her, Apollo had the baby brought to Delphi and raised to become a temple servant. Now, when the boy is already entering young manhood, Apollo bestows him on Xouthos as the latter's child. Kreousa, who does not know the truth about the child's identity, reacts to her husband's good fortune by trying to kill—as an interloper—the very son she has despaired of finding. The attempt providentially fails, but it is only after the boy in turn threatens Kreousa with death that the Pythia at last reveals the birth tokens that permit the mother to recognize and embrace her son. The child of Kreousa and Apollo will now shoulder his Athenian destiny, and Xouthos will be left content in the belief that the boy, whom he has named Ion, is really his own.

---

1. The date of the *Ion* is not certain, but metrical and other considerations suggest the period 412–410 B.C.

We, as audience, are let in from the very start on what otherwise only the gods know—who Ion is—and thus the sort of irony that has come to be called tragic from countless discussions of Sophocles' *Oedipus* (a play that shares the *Ion*'s underlying myth of the foundling's return) pervades the entire work. Only here, because the prologue also assures us that the ending will be "happy," the effect is more like that of comedy. In fact, the plot is quite similar to that of a comedy by a fourth-century playwright, Menander's *Arbitration* (*Epitrepontes*).[2] This helps to explain the unease many have felt about the play's genre, for it seems to oscillate between tragedy and something else, not comedy as fifth-century Athens understood it, but what was to become the comic tradition from Menander to Molière and beyond. This is not, of course, to say that the nature of the *Ion* is fully revealed by claiming it for comedy. Its plot, after all, is also reminiscent of innumerable accounts of heroic births and childhoods, for example, that of Persian king Cyrus in Herodotus' account.[3] And for all that it ends in resolution, the *Ion* again and again arouses a *frisson* through its near misses, intentions, and actions that almost end in disastrous overturns of fortune.

Later theories of genre notwithstanding, Greek tragedy in the later fifth century, especially that of Euripides, clearly welcomes such mixtures with open arms. In that respect, the *Ion* belongs squarely with Euripides' *Iphigeneia in Tauris* and *Helen* (two plays close in date) that also show features of romantic melodrama and depend on recognitions that lead to happy endings; but they also deal in serious ways with ignorance, violence, cruelty, and the threat of death as well as with the possibility of hope and of healing. It is precisely in the mixture of opposites, in an irreducible doubleness, that the particular genius of this play finds its expression.

The play itself provides a fitting emblem of its own doubleness at the midpoint, when Kreousa, queen of Athens, decides that the interloper Ion must be destroyed. To accomplish this, she produces a bracelet containing two drops of Gorgon's blood given by Athena to her ancestor Erichthonios: "One kills, the other cures" (l. 979). Kreousa wants to use only the lethal drop, and the healing drop is never mentioned again, but its presence here can hardly be a mere nod in the direction of the conventional etiology of Athena's aegis, which Euripides otherwise sets aside.[4] It represents a possi-

---

2. We possess something like two-thirds of *Arbitration* in fragmentary papyri. The plot is clear: A young woman has been raped by a rich young man, the baby is exposed but saved, and a recognition restores order by establishing that the father is none other than the man the mother subsequently married.

3. Herodotus *Histories* 1. 108–24. Cyrus, like Ion, is adorned in burial clothes, placed in a basket, and left in a remote place; brought up in a slave's family, he is eventually recognized, is reintegrated into his royal family, and fulfills his destined role as king.

4. See p.11 below.

bility that the play will realize at last (and in the nick of time) when Kreousa and Ion stand revealed to each other as long-lost mother and son. Kreousa keeps the drops apart, for she believes that "good and evil do not mix" (l. 991). The play shows that she is wrong; that in the world the two are always and inextricably linked, indeed, are often the same thing differently experienced, differently understood. As the elaborate plot unfolds, any claim to final certainty about good and evil is undercut. Kreousa's drops of blood—"a double gift from the goddess" (l. 984)—function as a symbol of a deep doubleness in life that the play painfully encodes and that becomes, as much as anything, what it is about.[5]

II

A characteristic form of doubling in the *Ion* is the repetition of the past in the present.[6] The story of Apollo's rape of Kreousa and the secret birth and exposure of their child in the cave is told no less than five times; different contexts and tonalities mark the successive stages of its progress toward fulfillment in the drama. Hermes, who saved Ion without Kreousa's knowledge after she had exposed her son, now introduces the action that will reunite mother and child. Ion's survival replicates that of his mother, lone survivor among Erechtheus' daughters, sacrificed by their father (ll. 266–69). His birth is symbolically repeated, with naming and birthday feast, and when at last he is united with his mother, he comes to feel that he has been born again: "Dear mother, I was dead once, now in your arms I'm alive again" (l. 1397). Kreousa, who set him out to die in her despair, again attempts to kill him; Apollo, who spared him once, saves him again. Similarly, the plot itself shows several crucial doublets: two consultations of the oracle, Kreousa's hindered by Ion and Xouthos' successfully concluded with Apollo's gift of Ion; two recognition scenes, the deceptive one between Ion and Xouthos, the genuine one between Ion and Kreousa; two attempted killings, Kreousa's of Ion and Ion's of Kreousa. Finally, the Pythia's appearance at the end of the drama to return Ion's birth tokens and send him on his way to Athens replicates—on the spot where she found him—her divinely guided decision to take him in as foster child on the god's behalf. Through the tokens, unwittingly—but once more inspired by Apollo—she restores him to his true mother.

As the *Ion* recounts a story of origins, familial and dynastic, its most

5. It is worth noticing how this doubleness is encoded for Greek culture specifically in the representation of gender. The monstrous Gorgon, whose look turns men to stone; the goddess Athena, virgin and warrior; and Kreousa, mother and (potential) murderer—all suggest the equivocal status of female subjectivity in the Greek (male) imagination.

6. For repetition as "the principal means of the play's construction," see Christian Wolff, "The Design and Myth in Euripides' *Ion*," *Harvard Studies in Classical Philology* 69 (1965): 169–94. Wolff's article remains one of the best general introductions to the play.

obvious and persistent doubling—indeed, multiplication—is that of parents, real and imagined. Ion, of course, is one of the Greek heroes (Herakles is the most famous) for whom the tradition claimed dual paternity, human and divine. Yet Ion can say as the play begins, "No mother, no father / watches over me" (ll. 99–100). For him, Apollo is only *like* a father, the Pythia takes the place of a mother, but his real origins remain hidden. Prompted by Apollo, Kreousa's husband, Xouthos, will claim Ion as his son and on Apollo's orders will be left with this illusion even as Ion comes to know that he is truly the god's own child. As regards his mother, Ion speculates that she was "a woman treated wrongly" (l. 314), and Xouthos, happily bemused to find he has a son at Delphi, recalls an earlier visit "for the torchlight mysteries of Dionysos" (l. 528) when he slept with a local girl. Kreousa's old retainer goes so far as to imagine that Xouthos deliberately "takes to bed some slave girl" (l. 788) after he sees that his wife will bear him no children and that he thus stages the trip to Delphi to find Ion by seeming accident. Only later, after Kreousa's attempted murder and Ion's threatened revenge, do hated stepson and stepmother find in each other the parent and child each has longed for. At that point, however, when Ion learns that Xouthos is not his father, he supposes that he must be the fruit of some secret, shameful love affair, and he refuses to accept Kreousa's word for Apollo's paternity. Only Athena's appearance *ex machina* stops him from confronting the god to "ask point-blank" (l. 1516).

The imagined doubling of parents implies, of course, a corresponding duplication of children. Ion becomes through Apollo's gift the son Xouthos never knew he had. Kreousa, who assumes that Apollo has abandoned their child to die, invents a fictitious double through whom she tells of the loss of a son just Ion's age. And only after attempting to kill the son she believes to be Xouthos' does she discover that he is the very one she lost.

Corresponding to this doubling of parents and children is a pair of opposing models of generation and birth that seem to vie for primacy within the play. A specifically Athenian tale of autochthony, birth directly from earth, defies the usual sexual model of generation, and this tension persists throughout the play.[7] Athenians in Euripides' day apparently still believed that they were an indigenous people, subject neither to invasions nor migrations; their early history, prominently featuring kings born from the

7. Autochthony has been much discussed in recent years in relation to the *Ion*. See George Walsh, "The Rhetoric of Birthright and Race in Euripides' *Ion*," *Hermes* 106 (1978): 302–15; Arlene W. Saxonhouse, *Fear of Diversity* (Chicago 1992), 76–89; and Saxonhouse, "Myths and the Origins of Cities: Reflections on the Autochthony Theme in Euripides' *Ion*," in J. Peter Euben, ed., *Greek Tragedy and Political Theory* (Berkeley and Los Angeles 1986). Of particular interest is Nicole Loraux, "Kreousa the Autochthon: A Study of Euripides' *Ion*," in John J. Winkler and Froma I. Zeitlin, eds., *Nothing to Do with Dionysos?* (Princeton 1990): 168–206.

soil itself, confirmed this and reinforced their pride in their racial purity. Tension initially arises in the *Ion* because only Kreousa—emphatically connected to the tradition of autochthony as the sole surviving descendant of earthborn Erichthonios—can perpetuate the royal line, through sexual union, of course, and the motherhood she so deeply desires. Xouthos, on the other hand, is an outsider, a Euboean whose military aid to Athens has won him Kreousa as a "war prize" (l. 287). Thus, when Ion appears to be his son but not hers, she attempts to kill one who might, as the king's son, wrest Athens from its indigenous ruling house.

The fact that autochthonous nobility in this story is invested in the female exposes the central political issues of racial purity and exclusivity to a particular kind of irony. Autochthony, although in itself suggesting the motherhood of Earth, functions in Greek myth largely to exclude the female element in the ideology of birth and birthright. An autochthonous Athens is first of all a city of male warriors sprung from earth, needing no human mothers and therefore not subject to the uncertainty of sexual generation. Yet the future of autochthonous Athens depends on Kreousa's bearing a child who will perpetuate the royal line.[8] With appropriate irony, the chorus of Kreousa's attendants invoke the virginal, motherless goddess Athena, "Delivered from the summit / From the head of Zeus / By Titan Prometheus" (ll. 435–37), in their prayer that Kreousa be granted a child.

A further irony in Kreousa's role as preserver of the autochthonous Athenian line is that by giving birth to a male heir who survives, she definitively removes reproduction from the sphere of woman to that of man. The motherless Erechtheus gave birth only to women, then returned to a chasm of the earth from which he sprang (ll. 266–71). Kreousa alone of his daughters survived and conceived a child by Apollo, but the baby was adorned for death and returned to a hollow in the earth (ll. 1458–61). The discovery that Ion was rescued will change the pattern; the boy is to become a man, beget children, and bring the Athenian line into the orbit of male procreation. Autochthony henceforth will conform to the model of patriarchy.

Beyond these ironies, the mixture of Apollonian and chthonian in Ion's blood that confers upon him his destiny as founder of cities and ruler of men also marks him out as radically impure, as a compound of beast and god—in short, as quintessentially human, as the hero he is to become. Ion, immersed in a dream of pure service of a god whose whole essence is purity, must come to accept himself as the product of that same god's violent lust

---

8. Loraux (see n. 7 above) 191–92 points out that ensuring a lineage to autochthonous beings, whose origin is not held to lie in sexual reproduction, is highly problematic. Kreousa's childlessness is thus a reflex of the larger problem of ensuring descent in an autochthonous line.

and as destined for future greatness. And he learns his origins only after he feels the murderous violence of which his own soul is capable.[9] Indeed, Ion's very existence belies the idyll of purity and simplicity that is his Delphic life, calls into question the Apollo of his devotions, the Apollo he dreams of as ideal father (ll. 126–31).

One further, equally crucial point about birth and birthright must be made here. The chorus, as they pray on behalf of their mistress, wish the same boon for themselves: "children of my own blood" (l. 466)—and the play presents this desire as universal. (For Ion, of course, it takes the form of wanting to know his true parents.) But the inverse proposition seems also to be universal: No one will want what is *not* his or hers. Apollo concerns himself with Ion's well-being solely because of his paternity. There is no suggestion at all that a more general (or less selfish) providence is at work shaping Ion's fate. Not surprisingly, Apollo understands the need to trick Xouthos into accepting Ion as his own. Although Apollo is god of prophecy, he fails to read Kreousa's heart or divine that she will feel the same way. The astonishing fact that Apollo's plans go awry is due to nothing more or less than Kreousa's unwillingness to accept into her home (and Athens' ruling line) an alien child while she herself still suffers from the loss of her own son and the pains of her subsequent barrenness. This is what brings her, with the old tutor egging her on, to the point of murdering Ion.

Only the Pythia, priestess of the oracle at Delphi, seems capable of loving what is not her own: the baby Ion whom she is horrified to find at the door of the temple, but then accepts "with Apollo's help" (l. 39) and raises as if she were his mother. The Pythia, after all, has sacrificed private life and family, and she is to that extent exempt from the interests and jealousies that move both gods and men. Her rescue of Ion is an act of loving kindness, the sort of pure caring, apart from ties of blood or hopes of gain, that in Euripides can illuminate even the most bleakly tragic scene (one thinks particularly of Theseus in the *Herakles* gently leading the hero back to life after he has slaughtered his own children). Ion has come to call the Pythia mother (l. 310), a name she gladly accepts "though it's only a name" (l. 1277). But the relationship cannot be understood simply in terms of human solidarity, for just as Hermes connects the Pythia's pity with Apollo's plans for his son, so she herself emphatically associates her nurture of the baby Ion and her saving of his birth tokens with Apollo's inspiration (ll. 1298–1301, 1309–12). Thus, the Pythia, without knowing how or why, salvages the god's secretive and nearly botched bestowal of Ion's birthright, cuts him loose from the imaginary idyll of her maternity, and sends him

9. I owe this suggestion to Professor Herbert Golder.

out into the dangers and promise of a life that befits a man, the life of the *polis*.

III

The fact that the play is set before Apollo's temple at Delphi is no doubt in the first instance a way of emphasizing the role of the god in the story,[10] but place functions in the *Ion* in typically multivalent and ironic fashion. The extraordinary *parodos* (ll. 164–225) casts the chorus as awed and delighted tourists seeing the famous sanctuary for the first time, with Ion as their local guide. There is nothing like it in extant tragedy; the closest parallel comes from a fragmentary satyr play of Aeschylus, the *Theoroi* or *Isthmiastai,* in which a chorus of satyrs describe images of themselves that they carry as votive offerings to hang on the temple of Poseidon at the Isthmus. If the origins of the scene are thus comic rather than tragic, that is entirely in keeping with Euripides' technique in this play.[11] What Euripides has the chorus see and interpret, and thus conjure up in our mind's eye, is a series of mythological scenes that show victory over monstrous creatures born of earth: Herakles killing the Hydra with the help of his companion Iolaos; Bellerophon mounted on Pegasos slaying the Chimaera; and finally the Gigantomachy, the great battle of gods and giants, with Athena brandishing her shield, Zeus his lightning, and Dionysos his thyrsus against the rebels. The theme and its treatment, not dictated by the actual temple decorations at Delphi,[12] suggest Apollo's triumph over Kreousa, whose descent from the offspring of Earth is emphasized in her subsequent dialogue with Ion. Kreousa is associated throughout the play with chthonian serpents such as the Hydra and Chimaera; like the giants, she finds herself in increasingly open rebellion against the Olympian Apollo. But the images bespeak not only violence, for the heroic defeat of monsters and the gods' suppression of the giants are for the Greeks—from the time of Hesiod onward—above all, emblems of the imposition of order and civilization on a chaotic and anarchic world. A similar constellation of ideas informs the loving description of another Delphic space shaped by art, the tent set up to celebrate Ion's "finding" by Xouthos, only to become the scene of Kre-

10. We know that Sophocles wrote a *Kreousa,* and it is likely, although impossible to prove, that this play dealt with the same subject as the *Ion,* preceded it, and was set in Athens.

11. For a discussion of the Aeschylean fragment in relation to the drama of Euripides, see Froma I. Zeitlin, "The Artful Eye: Vision, Ecphrasis and Spectacle in Euripidean Theatre," in Simon Goldhill and Robin Osborne, eds., *Art and Text in Ancient Greek Culture* (Cambridge 1994): 138–96, esp. 138–39. This article contains an illuminating analysis of the *parados* and other ecphrastic elements in the *Ion,* 147–56.

12. On this subject see Vincent J. Rosivach, "Earthborns and Olympians: The Parodos of the *Ion,*" *Classical Quarterly* 27 (1977): 284–94.

ousa's attempt to kill Ion.[13] The decoration consists of elaborate tapestries seized by Herakles when he subdued the Amazons: hangings that depict the harmonious order of the heavens but are filled also with equivocal images of monsters, of Athenian king Kekrops and his ill-fated daughters, and of a Greek fleet facing barbarian ships (ll. 1108–31).

Such depictions and remembrances of violence subduing violence underline the fact that Delphi in this play is ironically the scene of a rebellion against Apollo's power. Kreousa comes to Apollo's shrine ready to denounce him to his face for his violence, much to Ion's horror (ll. 351–67). The old tutor, when he learns that Apollo has given Xouthos a child and (as it seems) denied one to Kreousa, first suggests the mad revenge of burning down Apollo's temple (l. 948). The saner plan that Kreousa settles on will still, if it succeeds, produce pollution beyond all imagining by killing Apollo's servant (and, as we know, his son) in the sacred tent during his feast of thanksgiving. The Delphians condemn her to death by stoning for "conspiring to pollute / the precinct with blood" (ll. 1176–77). Ion, whose cult of purity is given charming embodiment in his shooing of the birds that soil the sacred offerings, threatens them with his bow, but does not shoot out of reverence for "message-bringers / from the gods" (ll. 160–61). And, indeed, it is a bird, a dove wandering free in Apollo's sanctuary, that the god prompts to drink the wine poured on the ground, thus exposing Kreousa's plot. Ironically, however, Ion threatens to cause pollution in turn by seizing Kreousa at the altar where she has taken refuge, thus giving herself "into the god's keeping" (l. 1236). The ironies of this scene are the culmination of all that came before. Kreousa, who denounced Apollo's violence and lack of care, now stakes her life on his protection. Ion, whose life has until now been dedicated to Apollo's service, doubts the justice of his dispensation. Despite Kreousa's claim of divine protection, Ion feels no pity for her, though he pities his absent mother (ll. 1225–26). But in answer to the reproach that she "tried to poison Apollo's child," Kreousa reminds Ion that he now belongs to Xouthos, whereas she is Apollo's (lll. 1237–40). Ion chastises Apollo for allowing a criminal to be his suppliant ("No stained hands / touch this holy shrine" [ll. 1267–68]) and is moving to seize Kreousa when the Pythia suddenly appears. The revelation she sets in motion of Ion's parentage is one that Athena later tells them Apollo would have preferred to postpone but permits to prevent them from killing each other (ll. 1533–39).

Athens, of course, as the origin and destination of virtually all the

13. For a detailed analysis and interpretation of the tent's representations, see Froma I. Zeitlin, "Mysteries of Identity and Designs of the Self in Euripides' *Ion*," *Proceedings of the Cambridge Philological Society* 35 (1989): 144–97, esp. 166–69.

characters of the play, is its other crucial place, equally mixed in its meanings. The emphasis on Athenian purity that, as we have seen, is focused around the autochthonous racial exclusivity of the Erechtheid line, has often been thought to appeal to local pride, but the *Ion* is notable for its absence of praise of the city and her institutions. Ion mentions Athens' democratic politics only to reflect on how as an immigrant he will be barred from taking part (ll. 565–78). Unlike earlier Euripidean dramas (such as the *Children of Herakles* and the *Suppliant Women*) that celebrate Athens as a refuge for foreigners, the *Ion* makes outsiders a source of undefined but powerful fears. Very likely this reflects the "enormous fear and consternation" (Thucydides 8.1.2) that followed on the disastrous Athenian defeat in Sicily (413 B.C.) and the subsequent Spartan occupation of Decelea, only about fifteen miles north of Athens and in a key position for controlling much of the Attic countryside. Athens had shown herself vulnerable, and waves of anti-Athenian feelings swelled within and without her empire. In this light, the treatment of "purity" in the *Ion* is deeply ironic: Fears of the foreigner almost lead to the death of the true native-born king. At the end of the play, Athens' patron goddess appears *ex machina* to establish beyond doubt Ion's paternity and set him on his future course. From Athena we learn that Ion's children will found the four Ionian tribes and that his half brothers, to be born to Kreousa and Xouthos, will be the eponymous ancestors of Achaeans and Dorians. Thus, the seeming vindication of autochthony itself argues against exclusivity and for a Panhellenic perspective. Athens' enemies and allies alike all share a story of mixed beginnings. Athenian racial purity is also associated with violence from the very beginning. As a race sprung from earth, the Erechtheids are naturally drawn into the orbit of the monsters figured on the temple and tent at Delphi. Euripides stresses the connection by associating Kreousa's magical drops of Gorgon's blood with the Gigantomachy (ll. 961–77). To do this he must ignore the usual and well-known version in which the Argive prince Perseus slays the Gorgon and bestow the honor instead on Athena in battle with the giants. Athena in turn gives the drops to Erichthonios, whom she pulls from the Attic soil and protects by twining serpents about him (commemorated in Ion's own birth tokens [1374–84; cf. ll. 18–22]). The Athenian site most often evoked in the play and most central to the action—the cave below the Acropolis where Apollo assaulted Kreousa and where their baby was born—epitomizes both by its nature as a crevice in the earth and by its association with legends and rites of the Kekropid past the mixture of splendor and violence that characterizes the *Ion*'s treatment of myth.

IV

Myth is the matrix of Greek tragedy, but few plays *use* myth as richly or as problematically as the *Ion*. The foundling's divine paternity is never put in doubt, even though none of the characters suspects it until the end, but its meaning certainly is. The claims of Apollo and of Athens are reconciled at last, but by a process that denies the possibility of simple, satisfying closure. Cognitive and emotional strains remain as the price of trying to live the myth and still be true to one's own needs and desires. Human knowledge is shown to be limited and unreliable, but in the interaction of divine and human wills the gods are also revealed to be ignorant, for they do not know the depth and intensity of human feelings. Although in the end Apollo reveals that he has saved his son, restored Kreousa's fortunes, and left Xouthos happy in his illusion of paternity, the plot itself is woven from the resistence of humans to the capriciousness even of divine benevolence. Divine power, fully manifest in the play's denouement, goes only so far in enforcing the standards of truth and justice that humans ascribe to their gods. The gods Ion longs for correspond to something we might recognize as a divine impulse in ourselves and to nothing else in the world. But just as the passions and weaknesses of humankind infect the gods, so the violent dissonances of the myths trickle into every corner of human life. Euripides seems not to challenge the authority of myth (as an earlier generation of rationalist critics argued) but rather to assume it for the sake of argument and then to tease out the deeply disturbing consequences of that assumption.

The issues raised by the treatment of myth in this play can perhaps best be traced in the outcomes and understandings that the various characters achieve. At one extreme is the old tutor, whose loyalty to the house of Erechtheus is such that he has neither questions nor doubts. Learning of Xouthos' newfound son, he leaps to the conclusion that the foreigner is trying to foist his bastard on the Athenian royal house (ll. 778–801). It is a fine specimen of sophistic argument from probability, it embodies precisely the charges that Ion feared from the Athenians (ll. 567–69), and it is disastrously wrong. And, although the tutor's concern is to defend Athenian purity as he conceives it, he first suggests burning down Apollo's temple and murdering Kreousa's husband before finally settling on killing Ion as the best available revenge (ll. 948–56). In spite of his decrepitude, when next we hear of him he is zealously carrying out the attempted murder (ll. 1136–48). Convinced by his own diatribe, sure of his own righteousness, utterly unscrupulous in pursuing his ends, the tutor leads Kreousa to plan the death of the same child she accuses Apollo of failing to save, the very offspring of the royal house for whose integrity she is fighting.

Xouthos, more temperate in judgment and certainly kindlier in intent, is equally bound by his certainties, equally remote from the mysterious possibilities of myth. He is treated as something of a comic character, becoming as it were the cuckolded husband who alone does not know that the child in question is not his. The decision to keep Xouthos in ignorance is Athena's (ll. 1566–69), no doubt in accord with Apollo's wishes, but the scene in which Xouthos appears suggests that his ignorance is also self-chosen. Although he has no knowledge of having fathered a child, when the Delphic oracle tells him that he already has the son he seeks, it would surely be unreasonable not to accept his good luck joyfully. Xouthos inquires no further, forgetting in his happiness even to ask who the mother was, as he tells Ion (l. 518). He will continue in the untroubled belief that Ion is his son, and we have no reason to think that he will give the matter of the mother another moment's thought. This lack of interest, signifying as it does that maternity matters less than paternity, in some sense validates the ideology of motherless autochthony, but when Ion naively suggests that the earth might have given him birth, Xouthos' wry reply, "Son, the earth doesn't have children" (l. 520), sounds at once like a critique of the myths that form the heritage of Kreousa's house and like common sense. The improbable world of myth is a reality in the play to which Xouthos, for all his being a son of Zeus, seems to have no access. That is suggested, too, by the tone of comic realism struck at the beginning of the scene when Ion repels what he apparently takes to be Xouthos' pederastic advances (ll. 495–503). The contrast with the sympathy, the half-conscious recognition of kindred fates, that characterizes Ion's meeting with Kreousa could not be more pronounced.

For Kreousa, of course, the world of myth is very close, dangerously so. Indeed, she is a figure overdetermined in relation to myth, both a Persephone—the maiden, her flower yet unplucked, raped while gathering flowers in the meadow—and a Demeter—the mourning mother wandering in search of her child. [14] Apollo's rape and the child she bore him are at the very center of her being, first as suffering and loss to be endured in reproachful silence, then as attempted revenge, and at last as recognition. Having experienced his violence, Kreousa awaited his grace, so she believes, in vain. But she has not yet abandoned all hope. Although apparently convinced that the infant she exposed is dead, she still has come to Delphi to learn whether he may be alive or whether Apollo will at least grant her a new child by Xouthos. Even after Ion prevents her from consulting the oracle, Kreousa explicitly allows the possibility of reconciliation to Apollo's past deeds if only he will grant her the child she craves: "But if he heals this wound, / I will accept it, because he is a god" (ll. 410–11). It is

14. This point is developed by Loraux (see n. 7 above) 199–203.

only when it seems that Xouthos has been given Apollo's favor and she denied it that Kreousa despairs of a miraculous change in her fortunes and turns to violence. Reasons of state dictate the death of Xouthos' son, but Euripides has arranged the dialogue between Kreousa and the old tutor to lay bare her more intimate motive: revenge. If she cannot attack Apollo directly, she can at least kill the child he has given Xouthos (ll. 945–53). Her weapon will be blood of the Gorgon that Earth bore long ago to fight the gods. In her anger she herself becomes something like a chthonian monster: "Fireblooded dragon snake spawned / by the bull-shaped river god" (ll. 1211–12), as Ion calls her. Kreousa's overwhelming emotion, her feelings of pain, loss, abandonment pent up for years and, now that hope is gone, unleashed, surprise Apollo and topple the plan Hermes revealed (ll. 61–63). Yet, in the end, Kreousa is not implacable, nor did she ever demand more of Apollo than he would give her. By giving him her child, he has finally healed her and won her praise (ll. 1576–78).

Kreousa's acquiescence does not, however, constitute a complete vindication of Apollo. About the god's role the most divergent views have been expressed, and in truth it would be hard to find a simple, satisfying answer to the questions: what does he represent? who *is* he? We must obviously keep in mind that Apollo is not strictly a character in the drama—though his nonappearance is in effect an event. His fathering of Ion fits a well-known pattern in which the (usually violent) satisfaction of divine desire engenders the founder of a city or clan. Stories of rape, even divine rape, have divergent and conflicting meanings in Greek culture,[15] but if Apollo raped Kreousa, that is, as Ion points out with sardonic emphasis, simply the gods' way (ll. 418–24). The Greeks regularly treated divine lust as honorific for its mortal objects and the offspring of these unions as heroes. Apollo may seem to have forgotten his son, but he has not. Hermes, who did his brother the favor of rescuing the child from the cave where Kreousa left him, assures us in the prologue of Apollo's continuing concern and announces the plan by which all will be made right. At the conclusion of the action, Ion has found father and mother with the god's help, and Kreousa her child. Even Xouthos is apparently content in the belief that Apollo has given him a son. Athena concludes the prophecies of glory for Athens that end the play with the suave comment, "Apollo has worked it all out perfectly" (l. 1560), and so, up to a certain point, he has. But whether the neatness with which all the threads are sewn up really cancels all the violence and fear that permeates the play remains open to doubt.

The doubt runs through the play at several levels. We have already

---

15. See Froma Zeitlin, "Configurations of Rape in Greek Myth," in S. Tomaselli and R. Porter, eds., *Rape* (Oxford 1986): 122–51.

spoken of the way in which Apollo's saving care for Ion, far from being attributed to some generalized divine providence or benevolence, fits a pattern of attachment to what is one's own, reversible at least potentially into hatred of what is not. We have seen, too, that Apollo's plan almost fails because the god who "chants forever what is to be" (l. 7) misreads the future out of an inability to fathom the intensity of human feelings, the rawness of human needs. It remains to turn our attention to Apollo's child, Ion himself, whose "life has been / one song of purity" (ll. 47–48), and whose innocent piety makes demands that the god cannot meet and calls into question the meaning of the myth whose protagonist he was born to be.

V

We first see Ion as he sets joyfully about his task of cleansing the courtyard of Apollo's temple. His every word and gesture breathe the innocence and purity of a devotee who lives apart from the world. If it seems incongruous for a tragic figure to wield a broom, Ion dignifies the gesture by his rapturous dedication. The broom itself is made from Apollo's laurel, gathered "where everflowing streams / burst from sacred myrtle leaves" (ll. 107–8); the lustral water is drawn "from the Kastalian spring, chaste / as these hands that serve the god" (ll. 136–37). If there is something faintly comic about Ion's brandishing of the bow and arrow (Apollo's arms) to shoo birds from the sacred offerings, Ion's earnest effort to maintain the precinct undefiled also ennobles the threatened violence. Above all, his lyrical monologue expresses a deeply felt kinship with the god he repeatedly refers to as father.

Ion's devotion is deeply unworldly, and it soon emerges that to the extent that he does not know the outside world, he cannot fully know Apollo or himself. Apollo is not merely the god of pure light, the singer, and prophet; and Ion is not his son only. Kreousa's arrival begins his necessary education. In the mutual sympathy of queen and temple servant before they know each other are the makings of the recognition scene that will take another thousand lines to come. But Ion is distressed by the woman's tears, ill omened and (in his view) wholly out of place in Apollo's shrine (ll. 230–34). And when he learns the reason for Kreousa's misery, he is at first reluctant even to admit that Apollo slept with a mortal woman, but eventually concludes that in his treatment of their child "the god was unjust" (l. 344). And, although he advises Kreousa that she cannot confront Apollo with his shame in his own temple, he is deeply enough disturbed by what Kreousa has said to consider doing so himself (l. 417).

It is worth noting that Ion's shock is not a matter of ignorance of the many tales of divine adultery; on the contrary, the fact that the gods so often violate the very "rape laws" (l. 427) that they enforce against men is precisely what distresses him. "Don't. Not you," he tells Apollo. "You have such power, / your power ought to serve what's right" (ll. 420–21). The fact of divine seduction, simply taken for granted in so many myths (including his own) is unacceptable to Ion because the gods' conduct contradicts the moral law they themselves have forged (ll. 423–24). Ion does not yet know that he is the fruit of such divine violence, and thus his words reflect the limitation of his knowledge. Yet he points to a fundamental incompatibility between myth and the world it describes, on the one hand, and the notion of justice that the gods enforce among men, on the other hand. It is the same incompatibility that led Plato, a generation after Euripides' death, to ban the old tales from his ideal state, and neither Ion nor the play can resolve it.

When Xouthos claims Ion as his son, the boy is reluctant to accept the seeming good fortune Apollo has bestowed on him because it will mean the loss of his unworldly happiness, of the "simple, painless, balanced" (l. 601) life at Delphi. That Ion is drawn to public life the whole speech (ll. 561–617) makes clear, but at the same time his sensitivity to origins tells him that the son of an immigrant king and some foreign woman can claim no political rights in Athens, that his very presence there will provoke envy and hatred. The loss of Ion's innocence is enacted here in reflections that are surprisingly contemporary in tone. Ironically, however, they are based on the false genealogy provided by Apollo. Ion is not, as he believes (and as Kreousa will also), extraneous to Athenian power. And as the true son of Apollo and Kreousa, he cannot withdraw from the violence that is part of his story since the moment of his conception or from the power that is his destiny. The fear Ion here expresses of his presumed stepmother (ll. 580–83) is followed almost immediately by her plot to kill him. Indeed, the loss of innocence culminates in the play with Ion's willingness to use violence in the very sanctuary that he here describes as an oasis of tranquility.

In the end, then, Ion's acceptance of his dynastic and political role brings with it, of necessity, the loss of Delphic isolation and peace, just as the acknowledgment of his true parentage brings with it the end of the idyllic illusion of Apolline purity. Ion's passage from the innocence of childhood to the responsibility of manhood is both a return to true origins and an abandonment of beautiful dreams. Ion's picture of his life as Apollo's servant makes clear what he must sacrifice when he shoulders his adult responsibilities: the simple contentment "all men want, / but lose in the asking" (ll. 610–11). Ion's unwillingness simply to accept, as Kreousa does, the conjunction of tales that reveal him as Apollo's physical son shows the depth of his longing for the pure god who was his (imagined) spiritual father. Could Apollo, Ion's Apollo, really have fathered him or does Kreousa merely "blame me / on a god, to save me from shame" (ll. 1491–92)? How could Apollo deceive Xouthos by telling him that Ion was his? In the end, Ion, who earlier told Kreousa that she could not force the god to speak, tries to do so himself to learn what Apollo has kept hidden, only to be stopped on the threshold of the temple by the appearance *ex machina* of Athena.

Athena's appearance is logical enough:[16] she is the right deity to reveal to Ion his Athenian future, to escort him as it were from childhood to maturity, from private ideal to public reality, from holy servitude in Delphi to heroic kingship in Athens. Yet she herself says that she comes in Apollo's stead. This has often been taken as a sign of cowardice on his part, but what did he have to fear from these mortals? What Athena says about Apollo's desire to avoid open blame (ll. 1525–27) reminds one of what Ion himself tells Kreousa when they first meet: do not try to make the god denounce himself in his own temple (ll. 358–67). Apollo's intolerance of blasphemy is well illustrated in his horrifying treatment of Achilles' son Neoptolemos in Euripides' earlier *Andromache.* In that play, Neoptolemos has actually returned to Delphi to make amends for having once demanded reparations of Apollo on account of his father's death. Orestes sows suspicion among the Delphians, and it is they who kill Neoptolemos, but a mysterious voice from the depths of the temple clearly marks the deed as Apollo's, and the messenger concludes his account by commenting that the god who is "judge of what is right for all mankind" has himself behaved "like a base man remembering an old quarrel" (*Andromache,* ll. 1161–65). As in the *Ion,* the god is shown to enforce one code and live by another.

Surely Apollo's absence has another meaning, though, like his absence from the prologue. Apollo is central to the drama, but is at pains to keep his distance from its characters and their emotions. He is unprepared for the intensity of the human feelings that his plan unleashes, and to prevent Ion and Kreousa from killing each other, he must reveal the whole truth to them in Delphi rather than wait until they arrive in Athens (ll. 1533–39). Humans act as reason and their passions dictate, but inevitably they are ignorant, and so their actions may have dangerous consequences. Gods, for all their knowledge and power, cannot always understand or respond to human needs precisely because they are not human. They intervene when and how they choose and for their own reasons. Is it any wonder that life as it is lived is so full of uncertainties, seems so subject to chance?

16. But it is characteristic of this play, and a chief feature of what one might call the formal exasperation of its ending, that the *dea ex machina* is in effect a doublet of the Pythia, once again (and now definitively) stopping the action at a moment when it seems about to go badly wrong.

VI

The contrasts of this play, with its mixture of violence and beauty, passion and irony, emerge most fully perhaps in Kreousa's extraordinary *monody* (ll. 826–95). The chorus, in open defiance of Xouthos, have revealed the (false) oracle that grants Ion to him, and to her nothing. After some initial outbursts of desolation, Kreousa stands silent as the old tutor indignantly caricatures Xouthos as a man who, like some Jason, has betrayed his wife and now conspires to smuggle his bastard into the palace under her very eyes. (The charge, repeated by the chorus at the end of the third *stasimon,* is particularly ironic in view of the fact that the child is really Kreousa's, not his.) He urges vengeance, a suggestion Kreousa will later make her own, but for now it is not Xouthos or even Ion but Apollo against whom she cries out. With hope of children gone, her thoughts return to that other wept-for child (ll. 835–37), and the tale she earlier told to Ion on behalf of a fictitious friend she now claims as her own story, filling it out in a rush of emotion with intimate details of lived experience. Most extraordinarily, the denunciation of Apollo, a veritable explosion of outrage and loathing, takes the form of a hymn of praise. [17] Apollo is invoked as god of music, and the rape itself is tinged with a golden sunburst and the gold of the flowers Kreousa was plucking (ll. 846–58). Even the hatred of Apollo she ascribes to Delos, where Leto gave birth to the god, seems somehow tempered by the beauty of the feathery palm and laurel that she pictures there (ll. 889–95). Violent emotion and the detached contemplation of beauty are mixed here as they are in the descriptions of the Delphic temple reliefs and the tapestries that cover the tent where the attempt is made on Ion's life or in the evocation of the great torchlight procession of initiates from Athens to Eleusis, which the chorus pray that Ion will never live to see (ll. 1045–60).

Beauty and violence are mixed in the gods and in the world, despite Ion's dreams of unmixed purity. In the end, for Ion, the mixture produces recognition and power, but successful initiation into a new phase of life also implies the loss of what went before. Discovering his real link to Apollo, Ion must give up the feeling of kinship to the god of intense purity and radiant truth he had always harbored within himself. And he must recognize his bonds to the earthborn monsters that rage violently against gods and men, for he discovers that their violence is also part of his inheritance. But Apollo has shown him that his future belongs to the city and to action. For Kreousa, Apollo offers the means of transforming shame and apparent abandonment into glory and continuing divine favor. For Athens, Apollo offers in his son the promise of patronage and the means for future domi-

17. See Anne P. Burnett, "Human Resistance and Divine Persuasion in Euripides' *Ion,"* *Classical Philology* 57 (1962): 95–96.

nance. But what all this shows is just that gods, like humans, love their own and care for them as they think best. Can it be said to constitute a theodicy?

Gods and humans differ in knowledge and in power. Gods may do whatever they wish with impunity. Humans are far more restricted, and the consequences of limits may be disastrous. In the *Ion,* Apollo prevents a disaster, the mutual destruction of mother and son, but the crisis results in the first instance from his withholding of knowledge from Ion and Kreousa and from his outright lying to Xouthos. He averts catastrophe only by abandoning the convenient compromise he had planned and revealing the whole truth before he intended. Such is the force of human feeling, even against that other, divine order of knowledge and power. But the efficacy of this force depends entirely on Apollo's favor for his son, on bonds of kinship, and it does not allow us to draw any easy conclusions about divine benevolence at large. As shapely as the *Ion* is in its patterning of melodramatic intrigue and recognition, it unsparingly withholds the moral satisfaction that, for Euripides, can no longer be made to attach to the enactment of myth. The special distinction of this play is precisely the way in which it brings the myth to its necessary "happy ending" without ever letting us lose sight of how complex, contingent, and confusing it is to live in, to live through myth itself. Within it, as without, mortals manage as best they know how, and for the rest must trust to chance, or the chance of a god's smile.

Durham, N.C.   P. B.
1995

TRANSLATOR'S ACKNOWLEDGMENTS

I studied ancient Greek as an adult for only two years, so I have never had the skills or learning to translate Euripidean drama on my own. I have relied heavily on what others have been willing to offer me, and they have contributed a lot, directly or indirectly, to this translation. The late William Arrowsmith helped to shape my sense of the meaning of the *Ion* and of Euripidean drama. Herbert Golder offered detailed criticism of several passages in earlier versions. Rush Rehm generously and patiently led me line by line through the Greek and along the way shared with me his impressive knowledge of Greek theatrical conventions. I'm grateful for all his help. At a late stage in the evolution of the translation, I benefited very much from Peter Burian's corrections, instigations, and suggestions.

W. S. Di. P.

ION

CHARACTERS

HERMES messenger of the gods

ION servant of Apollo's shrine at Delphi, son of Apollo and Kreousa

CHORUS of Kreousa's female attendants

KREOUSA Ion's mother, Xouthos' wife, daughter of Erechtheus

XOUTHOS Kreousa's husband

TUTOR to Kreousa, retainer of Erechtheus' household

MESSENGER

PYTHIA priestess of the oracle at Delphi

ATHENA patron goddess of Athens

A crowd of people of Delphi

Line numbers in the right-hand margin of the text refer to the English translation only, and the Notes at p. 87 are keyed to these lines. The bracketed line numbers in the running head lines refer to the Greek text.

22

Loveland Public Library
Loveland, Colo. 80537

Dawn. Before the temple of Apollo at Delphi. The temple is decorated with
images. To one side is a grove of laurel.

Enter HERMES.

HERMES Atlas! Bronze-backed Titan stooped forever
under the grinding weight of the house of the gods—
Atlas slept with a goddess and fathered Maia,
who slept with almighty Zeus and gave birth to me,
Hermes, the gods' lackey. I've come here to Delphi,
the world's core where Bright Apollo sings to men
what is, and chants forever what is to be.
There is a city—it has had its share of glory—
named for Athena of the golden spear. There shining
Apollo
took Kreousa, King Erechtheus' daughter, in wedlock,   10
raped her in a cave, under Athena's sacred hill.
Athenian lords call that place the Long Rocks.
Her father didn't know. Apollo wanted her
to bear the child, but in secret. When her time came,
she took the newborn to the cave in which Apollo claimed
her,
exposing it there to die in its cradle's wicker shell.
And yet, Kreousa honored ancient tradition.
When Erichthonios was born, pulled from the earth,
Athena twined two snakes around the infant,
placing him in the care of the daughters of Aglauros.   20
To this day, Athenian children wear golden coiled
snakes
at their throat. Thus, Kreousa,
swaddling her baby as best she could,
left him there to die.
  My brother Apollo called for me:
Brother, go to the earthborn children of Athens,
the glorious sacred city. Go to that cave,
get the baby with its swaddling clothes and cradle,

23

bring him to my shrine at Delphi, and leave him at the
                                                        door.

He is my son. I will take care of everything.   30
   Apollo Who Speaks Two Ways at Once.
I did what he asked, brought the basket here
and tilted back the lid so the baby could be seen.
When the horses of dawn ran across the sky,
the priestess climbed the steps and found the child
there at the door. Outraged that some town girl
dared to drop her bastard here and pollute the shrine,
she ran to get rid of it, but suddenly,
with Apollo's help, her savagery gave way
to pity. She nursed him, raised him, the temple's child,   40
and doesn't know Apollo is his father,
or who the mother was that gave him birth.
The boy doesn't know who his parents are.
   Growing up, he roamed free as a bird
around the sacred nest. As a young man,
the Delphian lords trusted him as steward
of Apollo's golden wealth. His life has been
one song of purity, serving the temple.
As for Kreousa, the boy's mother, she married Xouthos.
It went like this: War broke out between Athens and
                                            Chalkis,   50
Xouthos allied himself with Athens, Athens won,
Kreousa was his reward, though he's not Athenian;
he's Achaean by birth, descendent of Aiolos and Zeus.
Since then, they've planted the garden year after year
and still are childless. So they've come here,
burning for children. Thus Apollo,
never as forgetful as he seems,
controls their fortunes and draws them here.
When Xouthos enters the shrine, the god will give him
his own son, declaring Xouthos the father.   60
His mother will not know he's really hers
until they return to Athens. Thus Apollo's "marriage"
will stay a secret, and the boy will take his rightful
                                            place.
The god will name him Ion. Throughout Greece

he'll be famed as the founder of Ionia.
    For now, I'll hide here in the laurel
and learn how things work out. Here he comes,
with his broom, to make the temple shine!
I will be the first of all the gods
to name divine Apollo's son. ION.   70

                      Exit HERMES.
Enter ION *with temple attendants. He carries a broom
made from laurel, a bow, and arrows. On his head he
                           wears a garland.*

ION Dawn's gleaming horses raise
     the blazing sun above the earth
     up through air steeped in fire
     where light on light routs
     the faint lingering stars
     into the sacred dark.

     The peaks of Parnassos, untrodden,
     flare, smolder, and take for us
     this day's charge of sun.
     Smoke of desert myrrh   80
     rises to the rooftop,
     shrine of bright Apollo.

     Inside, the priestess sits,
     at the sacred tripod,
     crying to the Greeks
     songs Apollo murmurs in her.

                (*to temple attendants*)

     Go to the Kastalian spring,
     purify yourselves, bathe
     in its bright blessed dew.
     When you return, to all   90
     who ask about the oracle,
     let your words be pure and kind.

With my broom and sacred garlands
I will purify the entrance,
as I have done so many years,
calm the dust with water drops,
watch for birds that foul
the offerings, flutter them
with my bow. No mother, no father
watches over me. I serve   100
Apollo's shrine that nurtures me.

                    Radiant work
                    Day after day
              My broom of laurel whisking
                    Water kissed
                      Reborn
              Where everflowing streams
              Burst from sacred myrtle leaves
                    All day
                      I toil   110
              Sweeping clean the sacred shrine
              While the sun's wing soars

                O praise and bless
          Apollo   Healer   Shining One

              No work on earth as sweet
                As work I do for you
                    Leto's son
              Where your prophetic voice
                Sears the brilliant air
                My slavish hand   120
                My glory and fame
                      I serve
                  Not mortal men
                But undying gods
        My constant work all easy constant joy
            Phoibos   Father   Bright God
                      I praise
                  Apollo   Helper

        Nurturing lord
        I call by name   130
    Phoibos   Patron   Father

        O praise and bless
    Apollo   Healer   Shining One

            (*He puts down the broom.*)

Enough of that. Now, a little water
from the golden jar, to settle the dust.
Water from the Kastalian spring, chaste
as these hands that serve the god.
May I always labor sweetly for him,
or stop only if good fate comes.
No! Get away from there!   140

            (*He takes up his bow.*)

Stay clear of the golden roof.
Fierce, mastering eagle,
messenger of Zeus, your killing talons
rule the sky, but I
will kill you and all the others
that range down from Parnassos
to foul and pollute this holy place.
O red-legged swan
oaring across the air,   150
Apollo tunes his lyre
to your song. Go home to Delos,
or I will drown your song in blood.
My bow sings a different kind of song.
You may not build your nests here.
Go have your babies somewhere else,
by the gentle Alpheios, or the sacred grove
at the Isthmus. I won't let you poison
the sacred offerings with your filth.
I do not want to kill message-bringers   160
from the gods, but that is my work,

my service to Apollo's shrine,
my life's eternal source of food and care.

          Enter CHORUS, *admiring the temple images.*

CHORUS So Athens is *not* the only place! Look!
Images of the gods housed here, too!
There's Apollo, Protector.
           Fantastic! The light!
           It splits, peering
           above the face of Apollo's house.
                    Look at this.   170
                    Herakles, son of Zeus,
                    grabbing and killing the Hydra
                    with his golden sword.
                            And who is *that*
                            with the blazing torch?
                    It must be a story we tell at our
                                weaving:
                    Iolaos, sharing
                    Herakles' toils.

Over here! Can't you see it?
Bellerophon riding Pegasos,   180
killing the fiery Chimaera.
They're all tangled.
           How about *this?*
           Stone carvings,
           dragontailed giants
           fighting the gods.
                    Over there you can see
                    Athena shaking her shield,
                    that Gorgon snake-nest,
                    at the giant Enkelados.   190
                            Yes! I see Athena.
                            She is our goddess.
And here is Zeus, poised to strike
from afar, his lightning
blazing at both ends.
           I see it!

And Mimas
burnt to ash
by heaven's fire.
       And Dionysos! His wand   200
       wrapped in peaceful ivy
       kills another giant, son of
              earth.
       Roaring Bacchos!

             (*to* ION)

You there, may we enter the temple
barefoot as we are?

ION It's not allowed.

CHORUS   Will you tell us
something else?

ION What?

CHORUS   Does it really exist? Is it really here,
the navel of the earth, inside Apollo's
            temple?   210

ION Wreathed in garlands, and on each side are Gorgons.

CHORUS   Just as we've heard.

ION If you want an oracle from the god,
offer grain to the fire. But to go inside,
you must sacrifice a sheep.

CHORUS   I understand. We won't trespass.
What we see outside is enough;
it delights and charms the eye.

ION Look around as much as you like.

CHORUS   Our mistress said   220
                    we could look to our hearts' content.

ION   To what house do you belong?

CHORUS   A royal house, one
                    in Athena's city—
                    here's our mistress now.

                                        Enter KREOUSA.

ION   You must be wellborn, woman, whoever you are,
       as your bearing and manners show.
       Appearances are usually sound evidence
       of a person's birth and standing.
       What's wrong? Why are you weeping?   230
       I'm astonished—everyone else rejoices
       at the sight of Apollo's shrine,
       but you shut your eyes and wet
       those noble cheeks with tears.
       One look at the god's holy cavern,
       and tears flood your eyes.

KREOUSA You're a kind and sensitive child.
         You're a stranger, yet you ask why I'm sad.
         Seeing Apollo's house, I measured back
         an old memory. I feel torn   240
         between two places—my body is here,
         my mind elsewhere.
                              O why are women
         so miserable? And gods so vicious?
         What justice can we ever find on earth
         when the injustice of the mighty destroys us?

ION   Something's hurting you. Does it mean . . .

KREOUSA Nothing. I've taken my shot.
         I'll be silent. No need to dwell on it.

ION Who are you? Where are you from?
     What name do I call you?   250

KREOUSA Kreousa. Daughter of Erechtheus. My home is Athens.

ION A great city. Noble origins, glorious ancestors. How
                                             lucky you are.

KREOUSA I'm lucky in this, in nothing else.

ION There's a story we've all heard . . .

KREOUSA What do you want to know, stranger?

ION Your grandfather, Erichthonios, was born from
                                            the earth.

KREOUSA Yes. His noble blood hasn't helped me much.

ION Did Athena really pull him from the earth's womb?

KREOUSA Yes, with virgin hands. She did not give birth to him.

ION Just like the pictures of it.   260

KREOUSA She gave him to Kekrops' daughters, to keep him hidden.

ION But they opened up the cradle, looked inside

KREOUSA and bloodied the rocks when they jumped to their death.

ION Yes! And I wonder about another story.

KREOUSA Ask. I have time.

ION Did Erechtheus, your father, really sacrifice your sisters?

KREOUSA For Athens' sake, he had the courage to kill them.

31

ION You alone were spared?

KREOUSA I was a baby in my mother's arms.

ION And a rift in the earth hides your father?   270

KREOUSA He was killed by Poseidon.

ION And there's a place called the Long Rocks . . .

KREOUSA That! Why do you ask?

ION Apollo honors it. His lightning blazes there.

KREOUSA Honors? It did *me* no good.

ION You hate what the god loves most?

KREOUSA It's nothing. We share a secret, that cave and I.

ION Your husband? Is he Athenian?

KREOUSA No, not a citizen; he's an outlander.

ION Obviously wellborn.   280

KREOUSA Xouthos, born of Aiolos, son of Zeus.

ION Can a foreigner marry an Athenian?

KREOUSA There's a city neighboring Athens—Euboea.

ION The sea marks its boundaries.

KREOUSA My husband helped Athens to sack it.

ION And you were his reward?

KREOUSA His war prize.

ION You're here without him?

KREOUSA With him, but he stopped at the shrine of Trophonios.

ION To look around, or to get an answer?   290

KREOUSA Just one word, from Trophonios and Apollo.

ION About crops? About children?

KREOUSA We're childless, after years of trying.

ION You've never had children? Not even one?

KREOUSA Apollo knows I have no children.

ION Poor woman, lucky in so many ways, unlucky in this.

KREOUSA Who are you? Your mother must be a happy woman.

ION They call me Apollo's servant, and that's what I am.

KREOUSA Were you an offering from some city? Or sold as
                                                   a slave?

ION I know one thing: I am Apollo's.   300

KREOUSA Now *I* pity *you*, stranger.

ION Because I don't know who my mother or father is.

KREOUSA And you live here in the temple?

ION No matter where I sleep, this is my home.

KREOUSA How old were you when you came?

ION They say I was a baby.

KREOUSA Who gave you milk?

ION No breast fed me. But I was raised . . .

KREOUSA By whom? Your misfortune sounds like mine.

ION I call Apollo's priestess "mother."   310

KREOUSA How have you survived?

ION The altars feed me, and every stranger who visits the
                                                    shrine.

KREOUSA The poor woman who had you! Who was she?

ION A woman treated wrongly, and I'm her son.

KREOUSA You're fed, you're well-dressed . . .

ION I'm Apollo's slave, my clothing comes from him.

KREOUSA You mean you've never tried to find your parents?

ION I have no evidence to go on.

KREOUSA I know a woman who suffered like your mother.

ION Who is she? If only she could share my burden.   320

KREOUSA She's the reason I arrived here before my husband.

ION To do what? Maybe I can help.

KREOUSA To put a secret question to the god.

ION You can tell me. I might help arrange it.

KREOUSA Her story . . . No. I'm ashamed.

ION Shame is a lazy goddess; you'll get no help from her.

KREOUSA With Apollo. My friend says she slept with him.

ION Apollo? With a woman? No.

KREOUSA She had his child, too, and didn't tell her father.

ION Impossible. A man did it but she's ashamed to admit it.   330

KREOUSA She says no, and she has suffered terribly.

ION Suffered? She slept with a god!

KREOUSA She had his child, then exposed it.

ION Did it survive? Where *is* this child?

KREOUSA No one knows. That's why I'm here, to ask the oracle.

ION If the baby died . . .

KREOUSA She thinks wild beasts killed him.

ION On what evidence?

KREOUSA She went back to find him—he was gone.

ION Were there traces of blood?   340

KREOUSA She says not, and she combed the ground.

ION How long ago was this?

KREOUSA The child would be about your age.

ION The god was unjust. I pity the woman.

KREOUSA She never had another child.

ION But what if Apollo took him, then raised him in secret?

35

KREOUSA No right to act alone! He should share that joy.

ION Your story chimes with my own grief.

KREOUSA O stranger, somewhere an unhappy mother yearns
                                                    for you.

ION Don't lead me back to pain I have forgotten.   350

KREOUSA I'll be silent. Will you help me get an answer?

ION If I can. But there's some trouble with your case.

KREOUSA Everything she does brings trouble.

ION How can the god reveal what he wants to hide?

KREOUSA All Greeks share the oracle openly.

ION The god acted shamefully. Don't challenge him now.

KREOUSA But she suffers painfully for what happened.

ION No one will give you this oracle.
Apollo would punish whoever makes him seem,
even justly, wicked in his own temple.   360
Forget what you came for. No one should ask
questions that oppose the god. We can offer
blood of lambs, we can read the flight of birds,
but we beg for trouble if we force gods to say
what they're unwilling to say. Twist truth from them,
their blessings will be twisted,
although we gain from what they freely give.

CHORUS Different men suffer in many different ways.
Who among humankind ever uncovers
one real happiness in life?   370

KREOUSA Apollo, twice unjust to that unseen woman.
Unjust here, unjust there, you failed to save

the one you should have saved, your own child.
You won't use your prophetic gift to say
if that child thrives, or is gone with nothing left
to mark his memory. But that's how it must be,
if the god won't speak and I'm stopped from knowing.
　　　There's my husband, Xouthos, coming from
　　　　　　　　　　　　　　　　the shrine.
Be silent. Not one word of what we've said—
I might be held at fault for keeping secrets.   380
The story wouldn't unfold as we would like.
There would be trouble. Trouble, too often
it's all men seem to think we're good for.
Men mix us all together, evil women
with the good. Misfortune is our birthright.

　　　　　　　　　　　　　　　　Enter XOUTHOS.

XOUTHOS First, I greet Apollo, and offer him
　　　　my blessings. Then you, my wife.
　　　　Did you worry? I know I'm late.

KREOUSA It's nothing, it's all right, I'm glad you're here.
　　　　Tell me what Trophonius prophesied.   390
　　　　Will we both have children?

XOUTHOS He refused to guess at Apollo's will.
　　　　But he did say this: I won't go home
　　　　childless. And neither will you.

KREOUSA O Leto, Queen mother of Phoibos, bless our journey.
　　　　Let the pieces of our past dealings with your son
　　　　soon fall into place.

XOUTHOS So be it. Does anyone here speak for the god?

ION Outside, I speak for Apollo. Inside, Delphi's nobles,
　　　seated by the sacred tripod, will deal with you.   400

XOUTHOS Good. That's all I need to know. I'm going inside.
　　　　They say the common sacrifice, made for all like me

who came for oracles, has turned out well,
so I want to get my answer now. Kreousa,
spread laurel around the altars. Pray that I bring
good prophecies from Apollo's house.

XOUTHOS *enters the temple.*

KREOUSA So be it. After what he's done,
the love that ties me to Apollo
is changed. But if he heals this wound,
I will accept it, because he is a god.   410

Exit KREOUSA.

ION Why does this strange woman talk so wildly
against Apollo? She must really love her friend,
or else she's covering up something
that begs to stay hidden. Anyway,
what is the daughter of Erechtheus to me?
Not a thing. I'll fetch holy water and pour it
into golden bowls. I really must confront Apollo.
What is he *doing?* Rape a girl, then desert her?
Father children secretly, not caring if they live
or die? Don't. Not you. You have such power,   420
your power ought to serve what's right.
If a man acts badly, the gods punish him.
It's not right for you gods to violate laws
you yourselves have forged. Let's pretend,
for the sake of argument, that you
and Poseidon and great Zeus who rules the heavens
enforced the rape laws against yourselves.
What a price you'd pay! Your temples
would be empty, lifeless, barren.
It's not right to let yourselves go,   430
swamped by a moment's pleasure.
Or to blame us for copying what you
consider good. You are our teachers.

Exit ION.

38

CHORUS Born without labor
        Delivered from the summit
              From the head of Zeus
                    By Titan Prometheus
        O Athena
        We beg you
        Come to us   440
              Soar down
              Blessed Victory
                    From the golden
                    Halls of Zeus
        To the earth's hearth
              The world's navel stone
        Let the dance go round
        The sacred tripod
              Athena O come
              Tell Apollo what we want   450
                    Artemis   untouched girl
                    Apollo's twin
          Virgin goddesses
              Plead our case   our cause
                    For the ancient house of Erechtheus
        Let the oracle be straight and clear
              We've waited so long
                    For the great gift   *Children*

        Lush endless happiness
        Belongs to those who see   460
        Shining in their children
        Golden generations yet to come
        Sons protecting a house at war
        And bringing love in peaceful times

        Palace? Wealth? Give me instead
        Children of my own blood
              I hate not having children   I detest
              Those who think that's good
                    Let me have moderate blessings
                    Let me have children   470

39

O Pan!
Above your knitted caves
Near the Long Rocks
Three spectral daughters
Dance in wet grass
Before Athena's shrine

Flute song rises
From the sunless caves
Where you play your pipes
And where a wretched girl   480
Exposed Apollo's child
As blood-feast for birds

That was a bitter wedding
And I have never heard
In tales or at my weaving
Of any happiness
That ever came to children
Born of gods and men

Enter ION.

ION Women, still waiting for your mistress?
The temple is sweet with incense.   490
Is Xouthos still inside asking about children?

CHORUS He is. No sign of him yet.
Wait. I think someone's coming now.
The door's opening. He's coming out.

XOUTHOS, *leaving the temple, sees* ION *and approaches
him as if to embrace him.*

XOUTHOS Ah lovely boy! What a nice way to begin.

ION I beg your pardon? Please watch what you're doing.

XOUTHOS I want to hold you and kiss you.

ION What? Has some god made you crazy?

XOUTHOS I know what I'm doing. I want to kiss my dearest boy.

> XOUTHOS *tries to hug* ION, *knocking the garland from the
> boy's head.*

ION I belong to the god. Keep your hands to yourself!   500

XOUTHOS I claim what's rightfully mine.

ION You'll claim an arrow in your ribs if you don't back off.

XOUTHOS You run from the one who loves you most?

ION I don't negotiate with lunatics.

XOUTHOS Kill me, then. Burn my corpse. Go ahead, kill your
father.

ION Father? That's outrageous!

XOUTHOS Let me explain. You have to know the whole story.

ION Story?

XOUTHOS I'm your father, you're my son.

ION Who said that?

XOUTHOS   Apollo, who raised you, knowing you were
mine.

ION *Your* version of the facts.

XOUTHOS   Apollo's! The oracle told me.   510

ION Told a riddle and you got it wrong.

XOUTHOS   Nothing wrong with my
                                               hearing.

ION What did Apollo say?

XOUTHOS   The first person I met

ION Met?

XOUTHOS   Coming from the temple

ION Was supposed to . . .

XOUTHOS   Be my own son.

ION Son, or someone's gift?

XOUTHOS   Gift. The gift of my own son.

ION I'm the one you met?

XOUTHOS   The one and only child.

ION An odd coincidence.

XOUTHOS   Amazing, for both of us.

ION My God! Who is my mother?

XOUTHOS   That I can't say.

ION Apollo didn't tell you?

XOUTHOS   I was so happy I forgot to ask.

ION Then I was born from the earth—Earth was my mother!

XOUTHOS   Son, the earth doesn't have
                                               children.   520

ION But how can I be yours?

XOUTHOS   Let the god puzzle it out.

ION Why not work it our ourselves?

XOUTHOS   That's even better!

ION Perhaps you once had an affair?

XOUTHOS   When I was young and
                                                        foolish.

ION Before you took Kreousa?

XOUTHOS   Never since.

ION Maybe you got me then.

XOUTHOS   The time fits right.

ION Then how did I *get* here?

XOUTHOS   I have no answer to that.

ION Athens is so far away.

XOUTHOS   It's a real puzzle.

ION Have you been to Delphi before?

XOUTHOS   Once, for the torchlight
                                                mysteries of Dionysos.

ION Where did you stay?

XOUTHOS   With a Delphian, and there
                                                were girls from Delphi.

ION You were initiated, so to speak?

XOUTHOS   The god was in us all.   530

ION So you were drunk?

XOUTHOS   The pleasures of Dionysos can't be
                                                    denied.

ION That's when you fathered me.

XOUTHOS   Now, child, fate has found
                                                    you out.

ION But how did I get to the temple?

XOUTHOS   The girl must have
                                            exposed you here.

ION At least I'm no slave.

XOUTHOS   And I'm your father. Accept me.

ION I have no right to doubt the god.

XOUTHOS   That's more like it.

ION What else could I want?

XOUTHOS   Now you see what you need
                                                    to see.

ION I am son of the son of Zeus.

XOUTHOS   Yes.

ION You're really my father?

XOUTHOS   If we trust Apollo's word.

                                            (*They embrace.*)

ION Hello, father.

XOUTHOS   That word is all love.

ION This is the day

XOUTHOS   that fills me with joy.   540

ION Mother, whoever you are, I burn to see you
     Even more than before, to press you to me.
     But if you're dead, what's left for me to do?

CHORUS We share your happiness but want our mistress
        to have the chance for children,
        to brighten the house of Erechtheus.

XOUTHOS My son, the god spoke straight. He let me find you
         and brought us together. You have the father
         you did not know you had. I feel the same desire
         to find your mother; I, too, need to know   550
         what sort of woman she was. In time,
         maybe together we can find her.
         Leave this place, leave your homeless life
         at Apollo's shrine. Come share my intentions
         in Athens. My wealth and power are yours.
         You will be rich, noble, not sick
         with poverty and namelessness.
         Why so silent? Don't stare at the ground.
         There's something on your mind.
         Don't turn this father's joy to terror.   560

ION Things seen close up are not the same
     seen far away. Things in the distance glow and charm.
     I'm happy to find my father, but now
     I ask myself: What will life be like in Athens?
     They say Athenians are earth's children,
     all native to their place. I'd be twice afflicted,
     the bastard son of a foreign king. Powerless,
     I'd be a cipher. But if I join political life

45

try to *be* someone, the weak and poor would
                                            hate me.
Capable men who, keeping their own counsel,   570
avoid political life, would take me
for a fool who speaks too quickly
in a city filled with fear.
And public men, acting in Athens' interest,
can use the vote to shut me out.
That is how these things tend to be, father.
Men in power are primed to fight
their rivals.
                        Besides,
I'd be foreign goods in your own house.
Your wife is barren, she will feel all alone   580
in her grief, estranged from your good luck.
She will hate me, and with good reason,
and you would have to take her side. If not,
your household will be ripped apart. Women
stab their husbands to death and feed them poison.
And yet, I pity your wife, father. She's so wellborn,
she shouldn't suffer, as she grows old,
the disease of childlessness.
                                    And power—
power enthralls. All order on the outside,
but torment inside. Is it happiness   590
to wear out your life glancing left and right,
vulnerable on every side?
I'd rather live as a man in the crowd
than rule as king. A ruler learns to love
the worst of men, and must protect himself
from the best, since they are the ones he fears.
You say that gold wins out, that wealth is pleasure.
But the rich man, counting his gold, guards it, too;
all he hears is gossip and slander.
Such wealth is a task. I prefer a life   600
that's simple, painless, balanced.
   Please listen, father. What I had here was good,
time to myself, the dearest thing a man can have.
Nobody bullies me. No wild crowds.

A trivial thing, I know,
but people here don't push each other around.
To the gods I offer prayers, and comfort
to my fellow men, serving those who are happy.
People coming or going, I treat them all the same.
My smile is always fresh. What all men want,   610
but lose in the asking, is mine already
by nature and habit together,
in Apollo's service. Father,
when I think it through, I'm sure
I'm better off here. Let me live by my own lights.
The gift is the same. The joy of great things
looms in small things too.

CHORUS True words, but only if our lady sees,
somewhere in this, joy she can call her own.

(*to* ION)

XOUTHOS Enough of such talk. You must learn, my son,   620
to be happy. Now, to start things off,
I want a common feast here where I found you,
and proper sacrifice; we should have done so
when you were born. I'll present you
as my special guest—as an onlooker, though,
not as my son—and we will do the same
in Athens. I don't want to hurt my wife.
She's still childless; she would suffer too much.
When the time is right, I will prevail
on her to let you have the throne.   630
    And I will name you Ion. It fits the way we met.
Ion, the first I set my eye on when I came out.
So, invite your friends to the feast.
Say your goodbyes, then leave this city of Delphi.

(*to* CHORUS)

And you, not a word. Absolute silence.
One word of this to my wife and I'll have you killed.

Exit XOUTHOS.

ION I'll go. But one thing's missing.
Until I find my mother, my life rings hollow.
O father, if only she were Athenian,
then I could speak out as I want.   640
A foreigner, coming to a pure city,
might call himself a citizen and think
he belongs. But his tongue's a slave.
He doesn't have the right to speak his mind.

Exit ION.

CHORUS   Shrieks, cries, I see more, worse,
to come. Her husband with his own son,
and she barren, left all alone.

Wrecked harmonies break
from your prophetic song,
O Leto's child, Apollo.   650

And what of this boy?
Raised around the temple,
who *is* he?

What womb held him? The oracle
sounds false; I dread to think
where it will lead.

Strange oracle bearing
strange things; the boy
has some cunning and chance.
Why *that* child, an outsider born   660
of other blood? Am I wrong?

Friends, do we tell her?
Stab her with this news?

Her husband—with him
she shared it all, every hope.

Now, as he learns to be happy,
she drowns in all that happens,

fading into old age
while he neglects her.

Did he share? No. He took.   670
Took wife, wealth, palace.

Outlander from the start.
Let him *die.* He robs my queen.

May he suffer worse than she.
        Let the gods turn back his prayers
                and his offerings burn barren, unsavored.

She is the one we love.
The king makes sacrifice and feast—
a new father for a new son.

                Up there! The wine god ramping   680
                on the mountain crag,
                his pine torch blazing both ends
                for his wild ones to follow,
                        their slender feet
                        dancing through the night . . .

                Parnassos! Let the boy die here.
                Don't let him come to Athens.
                Our city doesn't need this foreigner.
                To survive, we only need
                        the pure untainted   690
                        bloodline of Erechtheus.

        Enter KREOUSA *with* TUTOR. *She helps him make his*
                                                        way.

KREOUSA Old man, my father Erechtheus chose you long ago
         to be his children's guardian. Now we'll learn

what Apollo Who Speaks Two Ways has prophesied.
Come along, if you can. It's good to share good news
with a friend. If the prophecy turns ugly,
in your kind eyes I'll find sweet consolation.
You served my father well. Though I'm your queen,
I'll show you every kindness in return.

TUTOR   Daughter, your father would be proud.   700
You're noble, just as he was,
truly one of Earth's children.
But don't let go. Help me up a bit.
We must all *ascend* to prophecy. These old legs
need someone to share their work.
Young help is the perfect cure.

KREOUSA   Careful, watch your step.

TUTOR   Slow down, child.
My mind works faster than my feet.

KREOUSA   Use your stick, lean on it.   710

TUTOR   It's like me, it doesn't see too well.

KREOUSA   True, but don't give up.

TUTOR   Not willingly, but I can't use what I don't have.

(*to* CHORUS)

KREOUSA   Women! Like sisters we've shared stories
at the loom. Tell me, then, what the oracle
told my husband about children.
Give me good news, and you'll find
I don't forget those who treat me well.

CHORUS   O god!

TUTOR   A bad beginning.   720

50

CHORUS Poor woman!

TUTOR Bad things in store, for all of us.

CHORUS What to do? Death waits for us.

KREOUSA There's fear in this song.

CHORUS Do we speak? Keep silent? What do we do?

KREOUSA Speak. You have something for me.

CHORUS It must be said, though I die twice for telling.
There is for you, dear lady, no child to take
into your arms and hold to your breast.

KREOUSA Then let me die. ·   730

TUTOR Dear daughter . . .

KREOUSA   Pure pain
shrieks in me.
It must end here.

TUTOR Child.

KREOUSA   *Ai   Ai*
Grief stabs
my heart.

TUTOR Don't cry out yet.

KREOUSA   The grief is here.   740

TUTOR Not till we know . . .

KREOUSA   What's left to know?

TUTOR Whether your husband shares the grief,
or if you suffer alone.

51

CHORUS Apollo gave *him* a son, old man—
        a private joy that cuts her off.

KREOUSA   Evil, and worse, worse yet
               rips through me with every word.

TUTOR   This "son" you mentioned, is he waiting
        for a mother, or is he born already?   750

CHORUS Already born, and grown,
        Apollo's gift. We saw it all.

KREOUSA   What? Unspeakable!
               Don't tell me that.
               It scalds my ears.

TUTOR   Tell me clearly now, precisely,
        what the oracle said, and who the child is.

CHORUS The first one seen, the first your husband met,
        leaving the shrine—he was the son, the god's gift.

KREOUSA   No! And *my* child?   760
               I'll be barren, bereft,
               childless, alone in my house.

TUTOR   What happened then? Whom did he meet?
        Did he see anyone when he came out?

CHORUS Remember, my queen, the young man
        sweeping the temple? He is the child.

KREOUSA   If I could soar from this earth, this Greece,
               through the light-steeped air
               to far fields of western stars . . .
               O friends, I'm torn too much by grief.   770

TUTOR   His name. What name did his father give him?
        Has the oracle revealed that, too?

CHORUS Ion. Because he was the first one seen.

TUTOR And the mother?

CHORUS   That I can't say.
I do know they've gone to make a birthday offering
in the sacred tent. Your husband took the boy, in
                                                secret.
He plans a sacrifice and public feast for his new son.

TUTOR We've been betrayed, both of us, by your husband.
He has designed events to serve himself
and force us from your father's ancient house.   780
My love for you outsteps my old regard for him.
The facts speak for themselves: He came to Athens
a foreigner, full of promise; by marrying you,
he took up your inheritance. But soon he began
to sleep with other women, begetting children,
and all in secret. In *secret,* because he sees
you can't have children, and he won't share that
                                                affliction.
So he takes to bed some slave girl, who bears
                                                his child,
who he then gives over to a friend in Delphi.
Nameless, bred in hiding, the boy grows up   790
like a sacred beast on holy ground until, finally,
your husband persuades you to come to Delphi
because you're still childless. By now, the boy
                                                is grown.
It's not the god who lied, it's your husband,
patient all these years while he spun his web.
If we expose his treachery here, he'll simply
blame the god. But if he makes it back to Athens,
he'll contrive to bring his son to power.
And that name! A travesty of origins—
"Ion." The first he set his eye on!   800
There's no "first" here, just an old conspiracy.

CHORUS I hate clever men whose talents
disguise vicious intent.
I'll take my friends from simple honest men,
not from those too clever to be good.

TUTOR   The worst for you is still to come,
        when a slave's man-child, a nameless no man's child,
        is made master of your house. Your husband
        had another choice, bad though it was—
        he could have said *We need a son, of a freeborn*
                                                    woman.   810
        You're barren; I can save the house. If you refused,
        he could have married one of his own kind.
        Now *you* must act. Act as any woman should.
        Kill your husband. Sword, poison, deceit, anything.
        Kill the youngster, too. But do it now,
        before they murder you. Bitter enemies
        can never share the same house.
        I'll share the work, and the bloodshed.
        I'll go now where they're feasting.
        Live or die, I'll repay all the kindness   820
        you have shown me. A slave's disgrace
        lies only in his name. In virtue
        he can stand equal to a freeborn man.

CHORUS   We, too, will share with you what happens,
         either death or a decent life.

KREOUSA Silent still, Kreousa?
         Stop now and say no more?
         Or flood down light
         on that dark bed?
         What holds you back? Match   830
         your husband's shame with your own?

         My husband, traitor, robs me
         of house, robs me of children,
         hope's human shape, that hope
         now gone. Why silent about
         that other marriage, silent
         about that wept-for child?

         By Zeus' starry throne, by Athena,
         mistress of our citadel who reigns

at the sacred shore of Triton's lake,   840
I will not hide my marriage,
but heal myself and tell,
as tears flood my eyes and my soul breaks,
    how men and gods betrayed me,
    disgraced me in their beds.

        From seven strings
        strung between the bull's bright horns,
        you pluck soft songs,
        O Leto's child, Apollo.
        To sunlight's jury I cry   850
        my charge against you:
            Bright God,
        you came to me, sunburst
        in your hair, in the fields
        where I was plucking
        soft yellow petals
        that fluttered to my lap
        and sang back dawn's bright gold.
            Your hand grabbed and locked
            this pale wrist, dragged me   860
            to the cave bed, while I
            shrieked *Mother*. There you worked
            Aphrodite's shameless grace.
        In misery, I bore you a son.
        With a mother's terror,
        I put him back, left him
        to die on our dark bed,
        where you yoked me to darkness.
        Ah, I wept, alone. Now the child
        is gone, a feast for vultures,   870
        my son and yours.

    You
        Lord of song
        you all the while
            sing self-praise, you
            chant the future

before the golden throne
at the earth's core.
Into your ear
I scream these words: 880
Vile coward lover,
you forced me to be your wife,
now you give my husband a son
and my house to house him.
You owe *him* nothing. Our child,
mine and yours, you left to die,
prey for birds, stripped
of cradle clothes his mother made.
Delos, where your mother
labored you into life,   890
hates you. And the laurel
sprung up there
beside the feathery, bloodroot palm—
the laurel hates you,
seed of highest Zeus.

CHORUS The treasure hoard of evil opens.
It would make the whole world weep.

TUTOR Daughter, your face fills me with pity.
I feel I'm going mad—no sooner
do you clear my mind of recent trouble   900
than another wave of words shocks me,
surging away from evils we've just known
toward more wretched painful ones to come.
So, now, voice your charge against Apollo.
Who is the child? Where did you bury him?
Go over it for me once again.

KREOUSA I feel shame, but I will speak.

TUTOR I know how to share your sorrow.

KREOUSA Listen. There is a cave, on the north slope
of the acropolis, called the Long Rocks.   910

56

TUTOR I know it. Near Pan's shrine and altar.

KREOUSA I struggled there, it was dreadful.

TUTOR Say it. I'll grieve with you.

KREOUSA The Bright God forced himself on me. My miserable
                                                       wedding.

TUTOR I was right when I thought . . .

KREOUSA You guessed?

TUTOR Your hidden illness. The sighs and groans.

KREOUSA Now I can reveal my secret.

TUTOR But how did you hide Apollo's "marriage"?

KREOUSA Can you bear to hear it? I had his child.   920

TUTOR Where? Did you labor all alone?

KREOUSA All alone, in the cave that watched him rape me.

TUTOR Where's the child? Child! You have a child!

KREOUSA He's dead, exposed to wild beasts.

TUTOR Dead? Apollo did nothing to help?

KREOUSA Nothing. The child grew up in Hades' house.

TUTOR But who exposed him? Surely not you.

KREOUSA Yes. I swaddled him, and I left him.

TUTOR Who else knew? Who went with you?

KREOUSA Misery, secrecy—they never forget what's hidden.   930

TUTOR Your own child, how could you just leave it in
                                          the cave?

KREOUSA How? With a torrent of words and pity.

TUTOR Ah, god,
          cold-hearted what you did, but Apollo did worse.

KREOUSA You should have seen him, his tiny hands reaching
                                          out . . .

TUTOR Hungry for your breast.

KREOUSA That place was his, and I denied it. How I wronged
                                          him.

TUTOR You must have somehow hoped . . .

KREOUSA that Apollo would save his own son.

TUTOR Our noble house—a storm breaks!   940

KREOUSA Why hide your head and weep?

TUTOR You and your father's name are doomed.

KREOUSA For mortals, life is change; nothing remains itself.

TUTOR No more pity, daughter, not now. Put aside this loss.

KREOUSA But what must I do? Events paralyze me.

TUTOR Pay back the god who first did you wrong.

KREOUSA I'm only a woman. He's a god!

TUTOR Burn down his shrine, oracle of the twisted god!

58

KREOUSA I'm afraid. I suffer enough.

TUTOR Then do what's possible. Kill your husband.   950

KREOUSA But he was, once, a good man to me.

TUTOR Then kill the child who stands against you.

KREOUSA Is that possible? How? It's something I would do.

TUTOR Your servants have weapons.

KREOUSA Let's go. Where do we get at him?

TUTOR Inside the sacred tent where he celebrates with friends.

KREOUSA Too much in the open. Besides, slaves are weak.

TUTOR And you're playing the coward. How would you do
                                        it, then?

KREOUSA I do have a plan, insidious, workable.

TUTOR I'm with you.   960

KREOUSA Then listen. You know about the war of the giants.

TUTOR Earth's children fought the gods on the great plain

KREOUSA and Earth produced the awful Gorgon

TUTOR to help her children fight against the gods.

KREOUSA And Zeus' daughter, Pallas Athena, killed the monster.

TUTOR I heard that story long ago.

KREOUSA How Athena skinned it, made it into a breastplate,

TUTOR her armor, called the aegis

KREOUSA because the eager Gorgon struck against the gods.

TUTOR What did it look like?   970

KREOUSA A breastplate linked with rings and rings of snakes.

TUTOR What has this to do with revenge?

KREOUSA You know Erichthonios?

TUTOR Your ancestor, sprung from earth.

KREOUSA When he was newborn Athena gave him . . .

TUTOR What? Say it, get it out!

KREOUSA two drops of blood from the Gorgon.

TUTOR Which have some power against men?

KREOUSA One kills, the other cures.

TUTOR But how could a baby keep . . .   980

KREOUSA In a gold bracelet, passed down father to son.

TUTOR Till Erechtheus died and passed it on to you?

KREOUSA (*revealing the bracelet*)
         I still keep it on my wrist.

TUTOR A double gift from the goddess.

KREOUSA One drop seeped from the hollow veins.

TUTOR What power does it have?

KREOUSA Repels disease, nurtures life.

TUTOR And the heartblood's second drop?

KREOUSA Kills. Poison from the Gorgon snakes.

TUTOR Do you mix them or keep them separate?   990

KREOUSA Always separate. Good and evil do not mix.

TUTOR O child, dearest girl, you have all you need!

KREOUSA With this the boy dies. You will kill him.

TUTOR *You* say where and how, *I* will do it.

KREOUSA In Athens, when he comes to my house.

TUTOR It won't work. And *you* criticized *my* plans.

KREOUSA I think I see the problem.

TUTOR Even if you're not the one who kills him, you'll
                                              be blamed.

KREOUSA The old story of the wicked stepmother.

TUTOR Kill him here, now, where you can deny it all.   1000

KREOUSA Yes, and savor the bloodshed sooner.

TUTOR And you can keep your husband's secret to yourself.

KREOUSA (*giving him the bracelet*)
         You know what to do? Take from my wrist
         Athena's ancient golden handiwork and go where
                                              my husband
         makes his secret sacrifice. When they finish eating,
         and are about to pour libations for the gods,

61

put a drop of poison into the boy's cup.
His cup. No one else's. Keep it apart, just for him,
who wants to rule my house. Once he drinks it,
he will never come to glorious Athens.   1010
He will die here, rooted to this ground.

TUTOR Hurry back to where you're staying
       while I manage everything here.

(*Exit* KREOUSA.)

Old as I am, blood still runs fast enough in me—
that much I have in common with the boy.
I'm on the side of kings, if I can hunt the enemy
and share the murder that drives the boy from
                                    our house!
When fortune favors us, the right thing is to be good.
No law or custom holds us back when we
kill enemies who would kill us if they could.   1020

(*Exit* TUTOR.)

CHORUS   Crossroads Queen, who guides all things
              that loom out on roads by night,
              Demeter's daughter, Queen of Returns,
                   guide through this noonday light
                        the brimming cup,
                        death's portion caught
              from the Gorgon's slashed throat.
                   Guide our queen's plot,
                   keep foreigners out,
                   let our city be ruled   1030
                   only by the children
              of the noble house of Erechtheus!

              If the boy's death goes unfulfilled,
              the moment's lost. If her sum
              of hope and purpose fails, she dies,
                   throat snapped by a cord

or heart pierced.
    Agony
poured upon her suffering,
    but death is change   1040
    at last complete.
    Never in the sun's light
    could she bear to see
others in her father's house.

Hymns sung to Dionysos,
dawn on the twentieth day,
torchlight rivering down
    from Athens to Eleusis.
    There celebrants
    dance round the spring.   1050
    Imagine Ion there,
    spying on the mysteries!
The shimmering sweep of stars,
    the dancing moon,
    and fifty water spirits dancing
by the everflowing river running down to sea—
    all hymn
    golden-crowned Persephone
    and Demeter
    terrible fruitful mother!   1060
    Apollo's beggar
    hopes to rule there
claiming everything we've worked for as his own.

    O Singers
    tell how women reign
    more pious than unjust men.
    Change your jangling songs
that cry *unlawful* and *unholy*
at a woman's love, a woman's bed.
Sing a new and grimmer tale: 1070
    tell what men do to us.
    The son of Zeus, oblivious,
    childless with our queen

                                        turns
                              toward some other,
                              shares another's bed
                              and finds a bastard child.

                                        Enter MESSENGER.

MESSENGER You women, where can I find the queen,
           daughter of Erechtheus?
           I've run all over town looking for her.   1080

CHORUS   You're one of us. Tell us what happened.

MESSENGER We're hunted, our queen most of all.
           The men of Delphi say they'll stone her to death.

CHORUS   What are you saying? Have they found us out,
           our plot to murder the boy, everything?

MESSENGER Exactly. And you'll be punished, too.

CHORUS   How did they know?

MESSENGER Apollo uncovered it. He saw right edging out wrong
           and refused to be defiled.

CHORUS   Tell us how he knew.   1090
           Tell it all, we beg you.
           Knowing will make it easier to die.

MESSENGER When our queen's husband left the temple with
                                        his son,
           thankful for the first sight of the newborn boy, he went
           to make sacrifice to the birth gods, up on Parnassos,
           splashing blood on the twin crags of Dionysos that
                                        gleam by day
           and flicker with torches at night. *Wait here and set up*
                                        the tent,
           the father told the son. *If the sacrifice takes too long,*

64

start the feast without me. He rounded up some calves
and left, while the boy went straight to work.   1100

He erected the frame—roofpoles, guylines, all that—
then dressed the tentskin over the bones. Not a tent,
                                                really,
but a billowing, broadbacked pavilion, measured off
                                                exactly,
"from the middle point," as the wise men say.
                                Foursquare,
a hundred feet to a side, huge enough to house all
                                        of Delphi.
Most of all he wanted the walls cambered just right,
to hold off noon's burst of sun, and sundown's sharp
spilled radiance. Then he brought out sacred tapestries,
from the temple's secret hoard. Dazzling,
fabulous bolts of cloth that Herakles, son of Zeus,   1110
seized in his war with the Amazons then offered to
                                        Apollo.
Draped high over the roofpoles, they made a second
                                        heaven,
a celestial cover, up there, where heaven musters
                                all its stars
in the circle of sky, while the horses of the sun,
chasing day's last light, drag the Evening Star behind.
There it shines! And night in its chariot rides forth,
dark-gowned, striding slow, the stars holding close.
And there, the Pleiades, good companions, ford the sky.
And Orion with his sword, poised midstride forever.
And the Great Bear, curling its golden tail round the
                                        polestar.   1120
And high in heaven's festive weave, the white full moon
fractions the year, carves the months with blades of light,
till the breeding Hyades, clear sign that steers the sailor,
are chased away, with all the other stars, by dawn's light.
He hauled out other stuff, strange Asian things to drape
                                        the walls.
Odd scenes, Greek ships locking hulls with the Persian
                                        fleet.

Monstrous creatures, half man, half beast. Horsemen
                                    running down deer
and spearing lions in the wild. At the tent door,
they hung an image of Kekrops, Athens' first king,
snake-king, flanked by his daughters—an offering   1130
from some Athenian. In the middle of it all
he placed a golden mixing bowl; and a herald,
very proud of himself, stood at the door
calling everybody in Delphi to the feast.
Soon the place was packed. The guests decked garlands
                                    on their heads
and ate to their hearts' content. When they had their
                                    fill,
some old man barged into the middle of things, fussy,
                                    madcap,
playing the role of wine steward. *Let me get the water
                                    bowls.*
*Wait! Let me wash your hands. Permit me to light some
                                    incense.*
Why don't I just clear away those golden wine cups?   1140
After dinner, when the music started and the flutes got
                                    going,
the large wine bowl was mixed and everyone held his
                                    cup.
Then the old slave shouts *Stop! Too small! These cups,*
they are surely too small. Let me fetch bigger ones.
Take your pleasures quick, I say. Big cups, big bellies!
When each guest has a big gold-and-silver cup,
the old man offers one to the young new master,
the brimming cup laced with poison. A gift, they say,
from our queen, that the boy might leave the light.
No one knew a thing. The boy raised his own cup,   1150
along with the rest of us, when someone—a servant, I
                                    think—
said something, a dark word, a piece of wrong speech
that the boy, raised on prophecies, took for an evil
                                    omen.
So he ordered a new bowl filled, and that first libation,

for the gods, he gave to the earth, commanding the
                                                    others
to do the same. Silence all around. A servant then
remixed pure water and the best wine in the common
                                                    bowl.
But then, a riot of doves, sacred and free to roam the
                                                    precinct,
came careening in. They swooped down where the
                                                    wine
soaked the dust, they dipped and wetted their beaks,   1160
the drops trickling down their feathered throats.
The wine didn't bother them, except for one that
                                                    alighted
at the feet of the new son. Its bonecage quivered,
it shook like a bacchant, it screeched words no prophet
                                                    could unlock,
while everyone, dumbstruck, stood and watched.
                              The young thing rattled
and died. Its blood-red claws and brittle legs sagged.

Ion burst from his place, bare arms flashing from
                                                    his cloak,
and shouted *You wanted me to drink from that cup,*
                                                    old man,
Who's trying to kill me? He grabbed the old man by
                                                    the wrist,
searched him, found the poison, but the slave, even
                                        under torture,   1170
held out a long time before he revealed the plot,
                              how everything
was meant to work out. The boy ran at once to
                              call all the people,
he addressed the lords of Delphi: *By the sacred Earth,*
                                                    this child
of Erechtheus, this foreign woman, our guest, tried
                                        to poison me.
The lords easily reached a vote: Kreousa will be stoned
                                                    to death

for plotting to kill the god's servant, for conspiring
                                    to pollute
the precinct with blood. The whole city's after her now.
                                            Childless,
already miserable, she races farther down misery's
                                    long road.
She came to Apollo yearning with desire for children.
                                            But now
she has destroyed herself, her own body, her hope
                                    for children.   1180

                                    Exit MESSENGER.

CHORUS No way out. No way to turn death
        back, fly free from it.
        All too clear. Snakeblood poison
        mixed with wine that flows
        from the grapes of Dionysos—
        shining too clear
        our own wretched lives
        like any sacrificial thing,
        and my queen stoned to death . . .

        If I could fly unharmed through falling stones   1190
            or hide within the shadow-folds of earth
        or race off in a chariot swift as wind
            or sail fast and sure to open sea . . .

        No help, no hiding,
        unless a god steals us away.
        O queen, what waits
        for you now? Will we suffer
        the evil consequence
        of the evil we have planned?

                                    Enter KREOUSA.

KREOUSA They're after me. I'll be slaughtered like a beast   1200
         for sacrifice. Condemned by the vote. Betrayed.

CHORUS We've been told the whole fateful story.

KREOUSA I got out just in time and somehow made it
through their lines. But now where do I hide?

CHORUS The altar, of course.

KREOUSA   What good is that?

CHORUS It's unholy to kill a suppliant.

KREOUSA   I am condemned by law.

CHORUS They have to lay hands on you first.

KREOUSA   They're close
behind,
and they have swords.

CHORUS   Quick, sit by the altar flame.
If they kill you there, your blood will be a curse
on all their heads. We must bear whatever comes.   1210

(KREOUSA *moves to the altar, sits, and wraps her arms
around it.*)
Enter ION, *followed by a crowd.*

ION Fireblooded dragon snake spawned
by the bull-shaped river god,
you tried to kill me, your nature
vile as those drops of Gorgon's blood.
Grab her! I'll pitch her off Parnassos,
the rocks will comb her hair while she hoops
and tumbles down. Some god smiles on me.
Before I went to Athens to become
my stepmother's victim, I measured up
your vicious hatred here, among allies.   1220
If I'd gone to that home of yours,
you would have caught me in your trap

69

then cast me down to Hades' house.
But nothing will save you now, no altar,
no temple of Apollo. I have no pity
for you. I pity myself, and my mother.
Though not here in the flesh,
her name is never far from me.
Look! Look at the monster,
weaving lies with other lies,   1230
who cowers at the altar,
as if that will set her free and clear.

KREOUSA I'm warning you. Don't kill me, not here.
For my sake, and for the god whose ground this is.

ION What could you and the Bright One have in common?

KREOUSA I give my body into the god's keeping.

ION You tried to poison Apollo's child.

KREOUSA No longer Apollo's. You are your father's son.

ION I've just become my father's son, I've always been
Apollo's.

KREOUSA You're not what you once were. But now, *I* am
Apollo's.   1240

ION *You* are sacrilege! Everything I did was holy.

KREOUSA You became my enemy, so I tried to kill you.

ION I didn't bring war to Athens.

KREOUSA You'd have torched the house of Erechtheus.

ION With a burning brand, I suppose?

KREOUSA You'd have lived in my house, taken it by force.

70

ION My father gave me the land he won.

KREOUSA What has the son of Aiolos to do with Athens?

ION He saved your city with a sword, not with words.

KREOUSA Allies don't lay claim to every city they help.   1250

ION You'd kill me for fear of what I *might* do!

KREOUSA To save myself, before you killed me first.

ION You're jealous. My father found me, and you have
                                        no child.

KREOUSA Do you steal homes from those who have no children?

ION Do I get no share? Nothing from my father?

KREOUSA Nothing but a sword and shield. That much is yours.

ION Get away from the altar, it's holy ground.

KREOUSA Go preach to your mother, wherever she is.

ION You'll pay the price for trying to kill me.

KREOUSA Butcher me, if you want, but you will do it here.   1260

ION At Apollo's altar? Is that your pleasure?

KREOUSA To torture Apollo as he once tortured me.

ION No!
All's terror if the gods make vile laws—
their unconsidered acts outrage good sense!
To let a criminal sit here at the altar.
You should drive them off! No stained hands
touch this holy shrine. Keep and protect

only those who suffer, falsely charged.
Don't give refuge equally   1270
to both the godless and the good.

(*He is about to grab* KREOUSA *when the temple doors
                                                      open.
The* PYTHIA *enters, carrying a wicker cradle.*)

PYTHIA Stop. Look at me, my son.
I stand outside the temple, leaving the sacred tripod
entrusted to me by Apollo's law.
I am the Bright One's prophetess, selected by all
                                    the Delphians.

ION Dear mother.

PYTHIA I like that name, though it's only a name.

ION You've heard how she plotted to kill me?

PYTHIA I have heard. But being savage, you act wrongly.

ION Why not pay back killers in kind?   1280

PYTHIA Stepmothers against stepsons—always the same story.

ION And still true. *This* stepmother . . .

PYTHIA No more. You must leave the shrine and head for
                                              home.

ION What are you telling me?

PYTHIA Go to Athens, under good omens, your hands clean
                                          of blood.

ION A man is clean who kills his enemies.

PYTHIA You're wrong. But there's a story you need to hear.

72

ION You know I'll listen.

PYTHIA (*Holding up the wicker cradle.*)
         What do you see?

ION I see an old cradle, with little garlands.   1290

PYTHIA I found you in it when you were a baby.

ION What? I can hardly believe this.

PYTHIA I kept these things in silence. Now I tell their story.

ION Why did you hide it from me for so long?

PYTHIA Apollo wanted you to serve him at the shrine.

ION And now he doesn't need me? I want more proof
                                              than this.

PYTHIA He gave you a father, so it's time for you to leave.

ION And you saved all these things?

PYTHIA The god's words are slanted light, they spoke in me.

ION What words? Tell me!   1300

PYTHIA To save this thing I found, until the ripened time.

ION To harm or profit me?

PYTHIA Hidden inside are your swaddling clothes.

ION My mother! A clue to the story.

PYTHIA It's what the god wants now.

ION An incredible day—one new thing after another.

PYTHIA Take it. Now work to find the one who bore you.

ION How? I'll have to look everywhere—all over Asia,
                                                    Europe . . .

PYTHIA That's for you to figure out. I nursed you,
    my son, for the Bright One's sake. Without words,   1310
    he told me what to take, what to save,
    though I never learned why. No mortal knew
    I kept these things, or where I hid them.
    I give these things back to you. Goodbye
    forever. I give you a mother's embrace.
      Look for her here. Ask yourself first
    if some unmarried girl from Delphi left you;
    if not, see if it was a girl from elsewhere.
    You know now all the god and I can tell.
    He, too, has a share in this.   1320

ION O gods, not this. My heart streams back
    to where my mother made her secret marriage,
    had me, sold me, secretly, never fed me
    at her breast, but gave me up
    to a nameless life, slave to the shrine.
    The god is good, but some shadow
    of what he does weighs hard on me.
    She and I, mother and mother's son,
    lost from each other. An infant's joy,
    a mother's loving comforting arms, lost   1330
    to me, those happy times lost to us both.
      The cradle, Apollo, I offer up to you,
    that I be saved from knowing what I don't want
    to know. If my mother was in fact a slave,
    let silence cover all. "O Bright God,
    I offer to your temple all these things . . ."
    What am I *doing?* I'm fighting the god's will.
    He saved these scraps of my mother's past.
    I can't escape this. My fate lies right here.
    (*opening the basket*)
    Sacred garlands, little nest, what have you kept   1340

hidden, wrapped up for me these many years?
Look! The wrappings around the shell look new,
cleanly plaited, nothing has rotted away.
Time has left no stain. Have you
come down, untouched, all these years?

KREOUSA A sign from the heavens, beyond my wildest hopes.

ION Quiet, you.

KREOUSA I won't be quiet. Don't preach to me,
for I see the shell where once I put you.
You are my child. You were just a baby,   1350
babbling when I left you there
by the Long Rocks, near the caves of Kekrops.
I'll leave the altar, even if it means I'll die.

          (*She lets go of the altar and rushes to embrace* ION.)

ION Grab her! Some god has made her crazy.
She's left the god's image. Tie her up!

KREOUSA Kill me, go ahead. Don't stop. I *will*
hold on to you, and these hidden signs of you.

                                    (ION *backs away.*)

ION Too strange. You, too, want to stake a claim.

KREOUSA Claim what's mine. Love owns what it finds.

ION Me? Love? You tried to kill me.   1360

KREOUSA I love you, my son. What more can a mother want?

ION Stop lying. I've got you now.

KREOUSA That's what I came for.

ION All right. This cradle, is anything in it?

KREOUSA The swaddling clothes I once wrapped you in.

ION Let's hear you name them, sight unseen.

KREOUSA If I'm wrong, I'm yours to kill.

ION Speak. Your boldness chills me.

KREOUSA Once, as a child, I wove a little thing.

ION Like what? All girls weave.   1370

KREOUSA Mine was unfinished, my first try.

ION I'm no fool. What was it like?

KREOUSA Gorgons woven dead center of the cloth.

ION O Zeus! What fate hunts me down?

KREOUSA Fringed with snakes, like Athena's aegis.

ION Look!
This is it, found like perfect prophecy.

KREOUSA Soft echo of my girlhood after all these years.

ION You were lucky once. Is there anything else?

KREOUSA Snakes. A golden clasp. Athena's gift   1380
that retells the tale of Erichthonios,
a reminder the children of our race still wear.

ION What is it used for?

KREOUSA Worn around the neck of a newborn, my son.

76

ION Here it is. I long to know a third thing . . .

KREOUSA A tiny garland of olive leaves, from the tree
Athena first brought to our city on the rock.
I put it around your head. Still green and blooming,
isn't it? Born of that first and purest olive!

ION (*embracing* KREOUSA)
Dearest mother, I see you, I touch your cheek—
pure joy.   1390

KREOUSA   O child, to this mother's eye
brighter than the sun itself
(may the Bright God forgive me)
I never dreamed I'd find you
but thought you shared the earth
and darkness with Persephone.

ION Dear mother, I was dead once, now in your arms
I'm alive again.

KREOUSA   To heaven's bright unfolding,
my joy sings,
shouts high and far.   1400
Joy I never imagined—
Where does it come from?

ION I'm yours, mother. I can't imagine anything but that.

KREOUSA   And yet I'm shaking with fear.

ION That holding me, you don't really *hold* me?

KREOUSA   I exposed my hopes
long ago.
O priestess, what hands brought
my own son to Apollo's house?
What arms placed him in yours?   1410

ION The gods did it. But as things come round,
may new happiness match our old despair.

KREOUSA   Child, I moaned and cried
as you were born. I wept
and pushed you out of reach.
Now my breath
warms your cheek,
the most perfect pleasure gods can give.

ION Your song is one we both can sing.

KREOUSA   No more, no more childless house,   1420
the hearth is lit,
the land has its kings,
the house of Erechtheus thrives,
blinks awake from night
and gazes toward the high bright sun.

ION Mother, he's here, too, my father. Let him
share the pleasure that I've given you.

KREOUSA   Child,
what are you saying? No.
Keep my secret.   1430

ION Secret?

KREOUSA   Someone else. Your father was someone else.

ION God! You weren't married. What does that make *me?*

KREOUSA   No torchlight streamed me to my bed,
No wedding hymns or dance
swept me kindly
to your birth.

ION *Ai* So I'm lowborn. But, mother, then who . . .

KREOUSA   By the goddess who slew the Gorgon

ION Please talk sense!   1440

KREOUSA   And who broods over the city's crag
                    where the sacred olive grows

ION Mother, no more lies. Talk straight.

KREOUSA   Where nightingales sing on the rocks
                    the Bright God

ION Bright God?

KREOUSA   Took me
          to that secret bed.

ION Apollo? The story's changing. This is wonderful.

KREOUSA   When nine months came full cycle, I labored   1450
                and bore you, Apollo's secret child.

ION I love what I'm hearing, if it's the truth.

KREOUSA   Girlish things, my loom's
                  vague wanderings,
          they had to do a mother's work.
          I never put you to my breast,
          never washed you with these hands,
                  I left you there
                  in a desolate cave,
                  blood-feast for birds,   1460
                      a gift to death.

ION A strange, awful thing for you to dare, mother.

KREOUSA   All tangled in my fear,
          I threw your life away,
          killed you against my will.

ION I tried to kill you, too.

KREOUSA Strange and terrible then, strange
and terrible now.
Stormwinds lash us, bad luck
churns on every side,   1470
then the winds change
and the sea lies calm.
Let it stay that way. The past
blew hard against us, but now
let's hope to run full sail before the wind.

CHORUS Here's proof: Let no one ever think, not ever,
that anything lies utterly past hope.

ION All these switchbacks of luck and circumstance.
One minute we suffer, the next we're healed.
Is luck some goddess who brought us to the point   1480
where you would kill me, and I'd kill you?
My god!
The sunlight's bright embrace today helps us
make sense of all that's happened. I've found you,
mother, dearest of all things to me; I'm glad
my origins were better than I thought,
but I still want to know the whole truth.

(*Drawing her aside so that no one else will hear.*)

I promise,
I'll bury all of it in darkness,
just tell me who my father really is.
Maybe, as young girls do, you fell   1490
into a secret love? No need to blame me
on a god, to save me from shame
by saying that Apollo did it
when it was no god at all.

KREOUSA By Warrior Athena, Victory Bringer,
who fought with Zeus against the earthborn giants,

I swear your father was no mortal man,
but Apollo, your patron, the god of slanted light.

ION How could he give his own son to another father
and say I was Xouthos' natural child?   1500

KREOUSA Not "natural," *given,* conferred,
though sprung from the god himself,
given as one friend might give
his friend a son to provide an heir.

ION Is the god telling the truth? Or does his oracle lie?
The questions trouble me, and for good reason.

KREOUSA Listen, here's what I think. Apollo did right by you,
placing you in a well-born family. As adopted son,
you're the rightful heir. But if the god declared himself
your father, imagine what you'd have lost! So, you see,   1510
he only wanted to help. Because I hid
our marriage and because I tried to kill you,
no one would ever believe you were mine and his.
He had no choice: He gave you to another father!

ION No, that doesn't work. I want the truth spelled out.
I will go inside his house and ask point-blank.
Am I the son of mortal man
or of the God of Twisted Light?

ION *turns to enter the temple but is stopped in his tracks
by the arrival of* ATHENA *from above.*

Up there! Where the incense rises,
a god's face where the sun should be!   1520
Run, mother. We must not look on things divine
unless the right time has come for us to see.

ATHENA Do not run from me. I am not your enemy.
I bring you good will, here, and in Athens,
the town that bears my name. From there I come,

sped down the road by Apollo. He thought it best
not to reveal himself to you, lest he be blamed,
in public, for all that's happened.
He sent me here to tell you this:

(*to* ION)

You are her son, born of father Apollo.   1530
He gives you to others whom he has chosen
not by blood, but to place you in a royal house.
He planned to wait until you got back to Athens
before revealing the truth of these things,
that you were their son—hers and Apollo's.
But all the god preferred to leave unsaid
has burst into the open; so Apollo had to intervene,
and save you both when you contrived
to kill each other. Now to fulfill the oracle
and bring things to a close, I have come here.   1540
So listen:

(*to* KREOUSA)

          Take this child home and make him prince
of Kekrops' land, for he's descended from Erechtheus.
And it is just that he rule my city, my earth.
And he shall be famous throughout Greece,
and four sons shall spring from one root,
whose names will become the Four Tribes
clustered around the crag which is our home:
GELEON   HOPLES   ARGADES   AIGIKORES
At the fated time their sons shall settle
island cities of the Kyklades, and coastal towns   1550
to strengthen Athens, and also along the twin shores
of Asia and Europe. They will be named IONIANS,
rooted in his name, and they will be famous.
Xouthos and you together will have sons:
Doros, father of the Dorians, whose city
will be famed in song; and Achaios,
who shall rule the land of Pelops all the way
to Rhion on the coast, and his name shall be the name

borne by a great people—the proud Achaeans.
Apollo has worked it all out perfectly.   1560
First he gave you good health in your pregnancy,
so that no one would suspect the secret.
Then he told Hermes to take the child, still dressed
in the clothes you swaddled him in, and bring him here,
where the god nurtured his son and did not let him die.

Absolute silence! Breathe not a word
of how you got your child. Let Xouthos cherish
his sweet illusion. Go, but keep this good news
to yourselves. Farewell. Be happy.
After all your troubles, I bring you news: 1570
Your fate, filled with the god, is blessed.

ION Athena, daughter of almighty Zeus, I cannot
not believe what you say. But I accept, I believe,
I am the son of her and the God of Various Light.
Even before, this was not unbelievable.

KREOUSA Hear me, too. I did not praise Apollo,
but I will praise him now, for he gives me back
the child he once ignored.

                    (*She touches the temple doors.*)

                              These golden doors,
once hateful, leering, smile now.

                    (*She embraces the door knocker.*)

                              I say goodbye
and cling to the god's bright doors   1580
that close him in.

ATHENA I commend your change from blame to praise of the god.
For the gods always work in their own good time,
and, in the end, they use what power they have.

KREOUSA (*to* ION)
> My child, let's go home.

ATHENA
>   Go, and I will follow.

KREOUSA Our safe conduct on the road.

ATHENA
>   I love my city.

KREOUSA Come claim your rightful power.

ION
>   For me, a worthy
>   possession.

> ATHENA, ION, KREOUSA *leave the theater, followed by*
>   CHORUS.

CHORUS Goodbye, Apollo, Son of Leto and Zeus.
> Now we have learned to give the gods their due
> and to take heart when we're driven by disaster.   1590
> In the end, the good get what's good.
> The bad, by nature, get what's bad.

NOTES ON THE TEXT

GLOSSARY

NOTES ON THE TEXT

1–163 The prologue consists of Hermes' speech (ll. 1–70) and Ion's *monody*—a solo aria accompanied by the *aulos* (a kind of oboe) and by the actor's dance steps and mimetic gestures (ll. 77–163).

3 *a goddess* Pleione, according to the mythographer Apollodoros, but Hermes does not name his grandmother and the tradition seems to have been uncertain.

6 *the world's core* A white egg-shaped stone at Delphi called the *omphalos* (navel) marked the earth's center, the place where two eagles, set flying in opposite directions by Zeus, finally met. For a description, see lines 209–11.

6 *Bright Apollo sings to men* The god known here and often by the cult name Phoibos, Bright One, is said to sing to men because oracles in verse were chanted or delivered to petitioners in written form by his chief priest after consultation with the Pythia whom he inspired (cf. ll. 83–86).

11 *raped her* Literally, "yoked in marriage by force." The violence of the union is emphasized repeatedly in the course of the play; see introduction, p. 13.

20 *daughters of Aglauros* King Kekrops of Athens and his wife Aglauros had three daughters, Herse, Aglauros, and Pandrosos, to whom Athena entrusted the baby Erichthonios for safekeeping. The story is told at lines 254 ff.

31 *Apollo Who Speaks Two Ways at Once* The cult name here is Loxias (Oblique One), which may originally have referred to "slanting" (riddling) oracles or to the inclination of the ecliptic traversed by the sun. Apollo is referred to by this name twenty-three times in the course of the play.

66 *I'll hide* Euripides gives Hermes, "the gods' lackey" (l. 5), the sort of exit into hiding just out of sight associated with conniving slaves in later Greek comedy.

152–58 *Delos . . . Alpheios . . . the Isthmus* Sites of important shrines, respectively, of Apollo, Zeus (Olympia), and Poseidon (Isthmus of Corinth). Ion's shooing of the birds to other sacred precincts to avoid defilement of this one gives his devotion a comic quality; at the same time his threat to shoot the birds to prevent pollution foreshadows his attempt at the end of the play to remove by violence Kreousa's "stained hands" (l. 1267) from Apollo's altar.

164–225 *Parodos* or choral entrance song. The chorus enter in three rows of five, led by a flute player, but soon divide into groups to dance and sing in wonder at the sacred images. The pictures they describe do not correspond to what we know about the sculptured program of the temple of Apollo at Delphi, although there was a Gigantomachy on the rear pediment. Euripides has rather chosen a series of scenes of victories of gods over monsters—appropriate to Delphi, where Apollo conquered the Python, connected to Athenian tradition (the same subjects were embroidered on the Panathenaic *peplos,* a ceremonial gown offered to Athena every five years), and above all appropriate to the themes of the play.

166 *Protector* Apollo is here identified as Agyieus, the divine protector of roads in whose honor incense as burned on conical pillars set before the street doors of Greek houses.

170–78 As one of his twelve labors, Herakles slays the Lernaian Hydra, a many-headed beast in whose blood he thereafter will dip his arrows. Iolaos, Herakles' nephew and bosom companion, appears at his side.

179–82 Bellerophon kills the Chimaera, described by Homer as "of divine race, not human, lion in front, serpent behind, in the middle a goat, and exhaling the fearful power of blazing fire" (*Iliad* 6. 180–82).

183–203 Battle of gods and giants (Gigantomachy). Earth-born monsters challenged the rule of the Olympian gods and gave battle on the plain of Phlegra (cf. ll. 961 ff.). Athena and Zeus are the most prominent Olympian defenders; Dionysos (ll. 200–203) was sometimes depicted in sculpture and vase painting as joining the fray with Silenos and satyrs.

226–433 First *episode.*

251–357 The longest passage in Greek tragedy written in strict *stichomythia* (line-for-line exchange). Usually used either for heated debate or rapid-fire interrogation, here its effect is intensified by the unrecognized conjunction of the tales elicited from each participant in turn and the unexplored convergence of their feelings.

254 *There's a story we've all heard*   As the mythographer Apollodoros tells it, Hephaistos, god of the forge, pursued Athena and, when she rebuffed him, his seed fell to Earth, who bore his child but gave it to Athena. Because the virginal Athena could not claim Erichthonios as her own, she shut him in a chest guarded by serpents and entrusted him to Kekrops' daughters with the injunction that they were never to look. They disobeyed and frightened by the snakes threw themselves from the acropolis.

266 *sacrifice your sisters*   Erechtheus' sacrifice was the subject of an earlier play of Euripides, the *Erechtheus,* of which only fragments survive. In that version, only one daughter was sacrificed, here all but the infant Kreousa were offered up. Erechtheus made the sacrifice at the behest of the Delphic oracle, who told him that only so could Athens win its war against Eleusis.

270 *a rift in the earth*   The mythographer Apollodoros explains that after Erechtheus killed Eumolpos of Thrace, a son of Poseidon, who had come to Attica to help the Eleusinians in their war with Athens, Poseidon angrily struck the earth with his trident, causing it to open and swallow Erechtheus.

274 *His lightning blazes there*   The allusion is apparently to a customary watch of three days and three nights for lightning on Mount Parnes, north of Athens. If lightning appeared, a public procession set out for Delphi in commemoration of Apollo's first journey there. (Strabo, a Greek geographer of the Augustan period, places the lookout at the shrine of Pythian Apollo, some distance from the Long Rocks, but Mount Parnes would be visible here also, and it is possible that the sighting took place here in Euripides' day.)

292 *About crops? About children?*   These are subjects about which Ion could easily guess that rulers might make inquiry, but they have a specific relevance to Kreousa and Athens; the notion of autochthony confuses crops and the children born from earth and are thus thought of as a crop (literally, "fruit of the earth").

298 *They call me Apollo's servant*   Ion still has no name, for no parents have yet named him.

324 *I might help arrange it*   Ion offers to be Kreousa's official local host and agent (*proxenos*); all those who wished to consult the oracle required a *proxenos* to introduce them.

395 *O Leto*   Kreousa prays not to Apollo, whom she holds responsible for her sorrow, but to his mother, who she hopes will understand her need.

425 *for the sake of argument*   Ion incongruously appropriates the language of the law court as if to prosecute the gods for rape. Ion in his idealism may intuitively feel that the anthropomorphism of Greek religious tradition is somehow unsatisfactory, but here as elsewhere he has no alternative way to understand the actions and motives of the gods.

434–88 First *stasimon*, a choral song (and dance) formally arranged in a series of pairs of stanzas connected by identical meter and music. The chorus in effect join the prayers for a royal child that Kreousa has gone to offer, directing their appeals to Athena, patroness of Athens, and Artemis, goddess of childbirth.

436 *From the head of Zeus*   There is irony in the emphasis on Athena's birth from the head of a single male parent, for the child who will appear as the result of the oracle for which they here pray will appear also to be motherless and to belong neither to Kreousa nor to the Athenian royal house.

442 *Blessed Victory*   Here a cult title of Athena, as again at line 1495.

456 *Let the oracle be straight and clear*   Again, there is irony: the Greek here speaks of pure (*katharois*) prophecies, but Apollo will lie to Xouthos and withhold the truth from Kreousa.

474 *Three spectral daughters*   Kekrops' daughters (see on ll. 20 and 254 ff.). Their story was reflected in a ritual observed in Euripides' day in which three Athenian girls who lived for a time in Athena's precinct carried a secret object in a basket down the acropolis at night by an underground passage, returning with other objects that they left in Athena's keeping. They were called Arrephoroi or Hersephoroi (dewbearers). It is presumably these girls whom the chorus imagine dancing before the shrine.

489–644 Second episode.

519 *earth was my mother!*   Ion, casting about for acceptable origins, unwittingly aligns himself with the Athenian traditions of autochthony that, indeed, lie behind his birth, for his mother is the child of an earthborn father and his birth, like that of Erichthonios (see l. 256), is the happy result of a seemingly unhappy encounter.

528 *the torchlight mysteries of Dionysos* Delphi was shared with Apollo by Dionysos, who possessed it during the winter months. Among the regular Delphic observances were ritual dances of female devotees of Dionysos, called Thyades, whose celebrations featured the waving of torches on the slopes of Mount Parnarssos.

537 *son of the son of Zeus* As Xouthos' son, Ion would strictly be Zeus's great-grandson; but as Apollo's he is, indeed, son of the son of Zeus.

632 *Ion, the first I set my eye on* In Greek the pun works off the participle *ion* (equally coming and going). Xouthos was coming out (*exion*) of the temple when he saw his new son.

635 *Absolute silence* But the chorus, surprisingly, will disobey; see line 727.

645–91 Second *stasimon.*

680 *The wine god* Dionysos, pictured leading the rout of Thyades in celebration on the slopes of Mount Parnassos; see line 528. The chorus assume that Ion was conceived at such a rite.

692–1020 Third episode, including a *kommos* (ll. 753–74, a lyric lament in which Kreousa sings all her lines and the tutor and chorus speak theirs in dialogue meter) and a *monody* sung and mimed by Kreousa (ll. 826–95).

727 *though I die twice for telling* This refers to Xouthos' threat to kill the chorus, who by speaking here strikingly breach tragic convention (cf. Euripides' *Hippolytos,* e.g., where the chorus keep their promise to remain silent and thus doom the innocent young hero). By reporting Apollo's oracle, the chorus spread the confusion that generates the rest of the plot. It should be added that they do so out of loyalty to their mistress and that the misunderstanding is not of their making, but entirely Apollo's. (There is, of course, irony in Kreousa's response at ll. 753–55, literally "unspeakable, unspeakable, unutterable the story you tell," because this is precisely the story they have been instructed never to speak.)

776 *the sacred tent* See line 1102.

810 *of a freeborn woman* References in fourth-century Athenian courtroom orations to an earlier law that protected freeborn concubines who were kept for the purpose of producing free children suggest that a childless Athenian might,

in fact, have imposed upon his barren wife an arrangement such as the one the tutor here suggests.

839–40 *who reigns/at the sacred shore on Triton's lake*   One of Athena's cult epithets, *Tritogeneia* (Triton-born), was most commonly understood to refer to Lake Tritonis in Libya as her birthplace (thus, e.g., Aeschylus *Eumenides* 293).

891–93 *And the laurel . . . bloodroot palm*   The laurel had strong associations with Apollo and is part of the Delphic scene in this play; the palm tree at Delos was sacred to Apollo because Leto clung to its trunk during his painful birth.

948 *twisted god!*   The cult name here is Loxias; see note on line 31, p. 87.

969 *the eager Gorgon struck*   Euripides constructs a punning derivation of aegis from the verb *aissein* (to strike) as a way of lending credibility to his version of its origin. In the usual story, Perseus gave the aegis to Medea after killing the Medusa.

1021–77 Third *stasimon*.

1021–23 *Crossroads Queen . . . Queen of Returns*   Persephone, the daughter of Demeter who returns to the upper world from Hades each spring, is here identified with Einodia, goddess of crossroads and patroness of sorcery. The identification serves the chorus' purpose by bridging the murderous work of poisoning Ion and the Athenian sense of exclusivity symbolized in the chorus by the rites of Demeter and Persephone at Eleusis, which they regard as justifying the killing of the interloper (cf. ll. 1029–32).

1045 *Hymns sung to Dionysos*   The Greek text mentions a "much-hymned god," presumably Dionysos in his guise as Iacchos, whom an Eleusinian ritual cry invoked.

1046 *the twentieth day*   This day of the Athenian month Boedromion was set aside for a great procession from Athens to Eleusis.

1055 *fifty water spirits*   These are the Nereids, sea nymphs who seem here simply to be part of a picture of all the elements celebrating the mysteries at Eleusis.

1078–1180 Fourth episode.

1102 *Not a tent, really* We are not told explicitly whether the pavilion was regularly raised for special occasions or was simply improvised for this one, but the construction and decoration now presented in such lavish detail suggest that it may have been a fixture of Delphic celebrations. On the other hand, Euripides' elaboration of the themes of order (in the tent's perfect structure and the cosmos depicted on its ceiling) and disorder (in the violence and confusion of the life depicted on its tapestries) offers sufficient explanation for the detailed description.

1111 *war with the Amazons* Among Herakles' labors was to bring King Eurystheus the girdle of Hippolyta, queen of the Amazons. The fabulous tapestries that Ion brings from the temple treasury are to be understood as booty won in that campaign.

1129–30 *Kekrops . . . flanked by his daughters* Cf. 254 ff. Kekrops' monstrous nature as snake-man is emphasized here in accrodance with the progression of images from the ordered heavens to the confusion and violence of earthly life.

1158 *free to roam the precinct* The doves thus form an ironic contrast to the birds Ion threatened to shoot for polluting the precinct (ll. 141–63), saving him from death and the shrine from pollution. Euripides images the flock of birds as a band of Dionysiac revelers, and in this context the dove that drinks the poisoned wine becomes a kind of substitute victim or scapegoat.

1175 *stoned to death* Public execution by stoning was a punishment reserved for particularly heinous acts of treason, sacrilege, or murder of an immediate family member.

1181–99 Fourth ode (in place of a *stasimon*). A short, highly emotional song that does not have the formal strophic responsion of a *stasimon*.

1200–1592 *Exodos.* This term, defined by Aristotle as the remainder of the tragedy following the final choral ode, obviously encompasses more than what we would regard as the final scene. In the *Ion,* the *exodos* includes two sudden and unexpected appearances, first of the Pythia (l. 1272) and then of Athena (l. 1519), and a lyric scene (ll. 1391–1475, the emotional recognition duo in which Kreousa sings her lines and Ion speaks his in dialogue meter).

1206 *It's unholy to kill a suppliant* Taking refuge at an altar made one the property of the god (cf. l. 1240) and therefore inviolate; anyone who killed or forcibly removed a suppliant from sanctuary would be subject to the wrath of Zeus in his role as protector of the rights of suppliants.

1212 *the bull-shaped river god*   Kephisos, the embodiment of a river of Attica, is here depicted in the form of a bull, a frequent feature of the iconography of river gods but particularly appropriate to Ion's emphasis on Kreousa's bestial inheritance from her earthborn ancestors. Kephisos was the father of Kreousa's mother Praxithea.

1272 *Stop*   The Pythia's surprising intervention is quite unlike conventional entrances from the scene building, whose central door usually opens only after an announcement, as at lines 493–94. This entrance is reminiscent instead of the sudden arrival of a *deus ex machina,* which in a sense the Pythia is. (For a human character in the role of a *deus ex machina* one may compare the otherwise very different entrance of Medea at Euripides' *Medea* 1317). All the more remarkable, then, that the Pythia's intervention does not tie up all the play's loose threads and that a second "god from the machine," this time the goddess Athena, is required to put in an equally sudden appearance at line 1519.

1373 *Gorgons*   The royal Erechtheid emblem, associated with Kreousa's attempt to murder Ion, now becomes a recognition token that unites them as mother and son.

1386–87 *the tree/Athena first brought*   In Athenian legend, Athena and Poseidon vied for primacy in Attica: Poseidon by striking the acropolis with his trident to make a salt spring flow there; Athena by introducing the olive tree. Athena won the contest and that first tree was said still to be flourishing.

1434 *No torchlight*   An important part of the Greek marriage ritual was a torchlight procession to lead the bride from her father's to her husband's house.

1445 *the Bright God*   The cult name here is Phoibos; see note on line 6, p. 87.

1498 *the god of slanted light*   The cult name is Loxias; see note on line 31, p. 87.

1510 *imagine what you'd have lost*   The world of the play here subtly shifts (once again) to contemporary Athens. The Greek literally says, "you wouldn't have had your inherited house and a father's name." Adoption law requires naming the biological father, and "son of Apollo" would not be suitable for this purpose!

1546 *the Four Tribes*   In classical times, the old Ionian tribes survived only for the purposes of certain archaic religious observances, but they no doubt retained a certain prestige based on their evident antiquity and derivation from the sons of Ion.

1554 *Xouthos and you together will have sons*   Euripides has changed the earlier traditions that made Doros the brother of Xouthos to bring both Dorians and Achaeans into Athens' orbit. His purpose in so doing has been variously interpreted. Athenian patriotism might obviously be at work in making Doros younger than Ion and the son of a mortal, but it would also seem possible that in underlining the ancestral relationship of Ionians, Dorians, and Achaeans, Euripides opposes a Panhellenic perspective to the Athenian exclusivity that dominates much of the play.

GLOSSARY

ACHAIOS: son of Xouthos and Kreousa, ancestor of the Achaeans.

AGLAUROS: wife of Kekrops.

AIGIKORES: son of Ion, ancestor of one of the four Ionian tribes.

AIOLOS: son of Zeus, who made him king of the winds, and father of numerous children, including Xouthos.

ALPHEIOS: largest river in the Peloponnese, flows past Olympia.

AMAZONS: a race of warrior women with whom Herakles, among others, did battle.

APHRODITE: goddess of sexual desire and beauty.

APOLLO: son of Zeus and Leto, twin brother of Artemis; god of prophecy whose oracular shrine at Delphi is the scene of this play.

ARGADES: son of Ion, ancestor of one of the four Ionian tribes.

ARTEMIS: daughter of Zeus and Leto, twin sister of Apollo; maiden goddess of childbirth.

ATHENA: patron goddess of Athens, born motherless from the head of Zeus; a virgin, she is associated with war, handicrafts, and wisdom. Athena's associations with Athens include the gift of the olive tree (by which she won her status as Athens' patron in a competition with Poseidon) and the raising of Erichthonios from the earth.

ATLAS: god of the Titan generation who carries the heavens on his shoulders; father of Maia and grandfather of Hermes.

BACCHOS: see Dionysos.

BELLEROPHON: hero who rode the winged horse Pegasos and slew the Chimaera.

CHALKIS: chief city of Euboea.

CHIMAERA: monstrous creature, part lion, part goat, part serpent; slain by Bellerophon.

DELOS: island at the center of the Cyclades, birthplace of Apollo.

DELPHI: situated on the lower southern slopes of Mount Parnassos, oracular shrine of Apollo, except during the winter months, when it was inhabited by Dionysos.

DEMETER: goddess of grain and mother of Persephone; worshiped at Eleusis.

DIONYSOS: god of wine and ecstatic possession, who inhabited Delphi during the winter months and led revels on the slopes of Mount Parnassos; also known as Bacchos.

DOROS: son of Xouthos and Kreousa (elsewhere Xouthos' brother), ancestor of the Dorians.

ELEUSIS: town in Attica, site of the mysteries of Demeter and Persephone.

ENKELADOS: giant who took part in a battle against the Olympian gods.

ERECHTHEUS: earthborn king of Athens, father of Kreousa and of other daughters sacrificed in order to win a war against Eleusis.

ERICHTHONIOS: earthborn king of Athens, grandfather (elsewhere great-grandfather) of Kreousa.

EUBOEA: island northeast of Athens, vanquished by Athens with Xouthos' help.

GELEON: son of Ion, ancestor of one of the four Ionian tribes.

GORGON: daughter of the sea gods Phorkys and Keto, killed by Athena (elsewhere by Perseus); from her blood Athena bestowed upon Erichthonios a healing drop; from the blood of the serpents that formed her hair, a drop of poison. From the Gorgon's skin, Athena fashioned the breastplate called the aegis.

HERAKLES: son of Zeus and Alkmene, hero who won deification through his many exploits, including battling with the gods against the giants and fighting the Amazons at the behest of King Eurystheus.

HERMES: son of Zeus and Maia, factotum of the Olympian gods.

HOPLES: son of Ion, ancestor of one of the four Ionian tribes.

IOLAOS: nephew and companion of Herakles.

ION: temple-servant of Apollo at Delphi, who in the course of this play discovers himself to be the god's son by Kreousa; future father of the eponymous heroes of the four Ionic tribes.

IONIA: the central part of the coast of Asia Minor and its outlying islands, whose settlement by Greeks Athens claimed to have organized and led.

ISTHMUS: the strip of land, properly the Isthmus of Corinth, that connects the Peloponnese to mainland Greece.

KASTALIA: sacred spring on Mount Parnassos near Delphi.

KEKROPS: earthborn first king of Athens, half snake and half man, to whose daughters Athena entrusted the baby Erichthonios.

KEPHISOS: the divine embodiment of the chief river of the plain of Athens, depicted in this play as having the shape of a bull; maternal grandfather of Kreousa.

KREOUSA: daughter of Erechtheus and Praxithea, queen of Athens; married to Xouthos; mother of Ion.

LETO: mother of Apollo and Artemis.

MAIA: daughter of Atlas and mother of Hermes.

MIMAS: giant who took part in the battle against the Olympian gods.

PAN: son of Hermes and a nymph; woodland deity worshiped the shrine of Apollo.

PARNASSOS: mountain on whose southern slope Delphi is situated.

PEGASOS: winged horse, offspring of Poseidon and the Gorgon Medusa.

PERSEPHONE: daughter of Zeus and Demeter, wife of Hades and queen of the underworld; worshiped at Eleusis.

POSEIDON: son of Kronos and Rheia, associated with the sea and other waters and with horses; killed King Erechtheus to avenge the death of his son in battle.

PROMETHEUS: god of the Titan generation who brought fire to humankind; in this play, said to have assisted at Athena's birth from the head of Zeus (elsewhere, Hephaistos is said to have opened Zeus's skull with an ax).

RHION: a city at the western mouth of the Gulf of Corinth.

TROPHONIOS: a prophetic spirit whose oracle was located in a cave fifteen miles from Delphi, just off the road from Athens.

XOUTHOS: son of Aiolos (and thus grandson of Zeus), husband of Kreousa, future father of Doros and Achaios (elsewhere Xouthos is son of Hellen and brother of Aiolos and Doros); banished by his brothers from his birthplace in Achaea, Xouthos became a soldier of fortune and won the house of Kreousa and the kingship of Athens by aiding in the conquest of Euboea.

ZEUS: ruler of the Olympian gods; father of Apollo, Athena, and Hermes (among many others); and grandfather of Xouthos.

LOVELAND PUBLIC LIBRARY

000284221

382.01
Euri-
pides

THE G

IN NE

GENERAL EDITORS
William Arrowsmith and Herbert Golder

Withdrawn

$7.95
4-28-97

DATE DUE

NOV 7 1997

GAYLORD			PRINTED IN U.S.A.